14-100-366

D1333164

Manual

FOR

Studies of Space Utilization

IN

Colleges and Universities

BY

John Dale Russell

AND

James I. Doi

Prepared for and in Cooperation with the Committee
on Enrollment Trends and Space Utilization
OF THE
American Association of Collegiate Registrars and
Admissions Officers

PUBLISHED BY

American Association of Collegiate Registrars and Admissions Officers
Robert Mahn, Chairman of Committee on Publications

OHIO UNIVERSITY, ATHENS, OHIO

PRINTED IN THE UNITED STATES OF AMERICA

GEORGE BANTA COMPANY, INC., MENASHA, WISCONSIN

AMERICAN ASSOCIATION OF COLLEGIATE REGISTRARS AND ADMISSIONS OFFICERS

OFFICERS OF THE ASSOCIATION
1957–58

President:

Roy Armstrong
Director of Admissions
University of North Carolina
Chapel Hill, North Carolina

President Elect:

Herman A. Spindt
Director of Admissions
University of California
Berkeley 4, California

Vice President in Charge of Professional Activities:

Ted McCarrel
Director of Admissions and Records
State University of Iowa
Iowa City, Iowa

Vice President in Charge of Regional Associations and Membership Promotion:

Clyde Vroman
Director of Admissions
University of Michigan
Ann Arbor, Michigan

Past President:

William Craig Smyser
Registrar
Miami University
Oxford, Ohio

Secretary:

Florence N. Brady
Registrar
Occidental College
Los Angeles 41, California

Treasurer:

E. Vincent O'Brien
Director of Admissions and Records
Fordham University
New York 7, New York

Editor:

S. A. Nock
Dean of the College
Cedar Crest College
Allentown, Pennsylvania

Member at Large, 1956–58:

Robert E. Hewes
Registrar
Massachusetts Institute of Technology
Cambridge 39, Massachusetts

Member at Large, 1957–59:

William F. Adams
Dean of Admissions and Records
University of Alabama
University, Alabama

COMMITTEE ON PROFESSIONAL ACTIVITIES

TED McCARREL, *General Chairman*
State University of Iowa

*ENOCK C. DYRNESS	*Wheaton College*
*S. A. NOCK, *ex-officio*	*Cedar Crest College*
*ROBERT E. MAHN	*Ohio University*
*ETHELYN TONER	*University of Washington*
*O. W. WAGNER	*Washington University*
IRENE DAVIS	*The Johns Hopkins University*
O. W. HASCALL	*University of Colorado*
JAMES K. HITT	*University of Kansas*
J. ANTHONY HUMPHREYS	*Wilson Junior College, Chicago*
J. EVERETT LONG	*West Virginia University*
D. T. ORDEMAN	*Oregon State College*
NELSON PARKHURST	*Purdue University*
A. TRUMAN POUNCEY	*State Teachers College, St. Cloud, Minn.*
ALBERT F. SCRIBNER	*Valparaiso University*
E. C. SEYLER	*University of Illinois*
HOWARD B. SHONTZ	*University of California at Davis*
CLAUDE SIMPSON	*State College of Washington*
WILLIAM H. STRAIN	*Indiana University*
ALFRED THOMAS, JR.	*Arizona State College*
R. F. THOMASON	*University of Tennessee*

* Steering Committee.

Foreword

By the Committee on Enrollment Trends and Space Utilization of the American Association of Collegiate Registrars and Admissions Officers

THIS volume, *Manual for Studies of Space Utilization in Colleges and Universities*, follows the publication of two reports concerning enrollment trends by the American Association of Collegiate Registrars and Admissions Officers. *College Age Population Trends 1940–1970*, first printed and distributed in 1953, and *The Impending Tidal Wave of Students*, published in 1954, were prepared by Dr. Ronald B. Thompson, Registrar and University Examiner of The Ohio State University. These reports, distributed widely, have been a major factor in stimulating action in the colleges and universities in preparing for the enrollments projected in the years ahead.

One of the basic problems facing institutions of higher learning is providing the plant facilities for the increased enrollments expected. Income producing units may be self-financed, but the enlargement of the physical plant for instructional space may present financial problems of considerable magnitude for most of our colleges and universities. The financing and construction of instructional units will not keep pace with the enrollment increases expected.

It is for this reason that the American Association of Collegiate Registrars and Admissions Officers turned its attention to the preparation of a manual so designed as to make it possible for college and university administrators to make a study of space utilization in their institutions. Such a self survey should lead to a better utilization of existing plant facilities.

A grant from the Fund for the Advancement of Education

has made it possible to publish this work. The Association wishes to acknowledge with thanks this generous financial assistance.

Dr. John Dale Russell, a distinguished educator, brings a background of over a quarter of a century of experience in higher education to this project. Dr. James I. Doi has applied a painstaking standard of research and scholarship in the preparation of the manual. The Association is deeply indebted to Dr. Russell and to Dr. Doi.

The Association is proud to present this volume to college and university administrators. It is our hope that extensive use of this manual will enable us to continue this study and to prepare a revision of the normative data based on a larger number of institutions. It is also our hope that this material will be utilized in a direct manner to the end that a better utilization of present instructional plant facilities will provide additional students with the opportunity of a higher education.

ALBERT F. SCRIBNER, *Chairman*
Registrar
Valparaiso University

CLARENCE E. DAMMON*
Registrar
Purdue University

ENOCK C. DYRNESS
Registrar
Wheaton College

LINFORD A. MARQUART
Registrar
National College of Education

JOHN M. RHOADS
Registrar
Temple University

KERMIT H. SMITH
Registrar
Michigan State University

RONALD B. THOMPSON
Registrar and University Examiner
The Ohio State University

June 1957

* Deceased.

Authors' Preface

IN May, 1956, the Committee on Enrollment Trends and Space Utilization of the American Association of Collegiate Registrars and Admissions Officers requested the authors to prepare a manual that would guide officials of college-level institutions in the making of analyses of the utilization of their plant space. The Committee sought and obtained a grant from the Fund for the Advancement of Education for the support of the project. This grant was supplemented by an appropriation from the treasury of the American Association of Collegiate Registrars and Admissions Officers.

To assist in making the *Manual* as comprehensive and as authoritative as possible, an Advisory Committee was appointed, with members drawn from a number of the national organizations in higher education. The members of the Advisory Committee were as follows:

THEODORE A. DISTLER, Executive Director of the Association of American Colleges

S. C. HOLLISTER, Cornell University, representing the American Council on Education

ERNEST V. HOLLIS, Office of Education, U. S. Department of Health, Education, and Welfare

W. T. MIDDLEBROOK, University of Minnesota, representing the American Association of Land-Grant Colleges and State Universities

JAMES E. REYNOLDS, University of Texas, representing the American Association of Junior Colleges

DONOVAN E. SMITH, University of California, representing the National Federation of College and University Business Officers Associations

The Advisory Committee met with the authors and the Sponsoring Committee in October, 1956, and discussed the general outline of the *Manual* and a substantial part of a first rough draft of the text. The members of the Advisory Committee gave valuable and much appreciated counsel, but they should not be held responsible for anything in the *Manual* that the reader may not find to his liking.

A special acknowledgment is due to Donovan E. Smith of the University of California for valuable consultative service to the authors in the preparation of this *Manual*. Thankful acknowledgment is also made of the courtesy of Dr. Thomas C. Holy of the University of California for making available a number of useful tabulations from analyses of plant space utilization. The counsel of James F. Blakesley of Purdue University is also gratefully acknowledged.

The sponsoring Committee of the American Association of Collegiate Registrars and Admissions Officers held a number of meetings, beginning in the spring of 1956, at which plans for the *Manual* were discussed and developed, and the text of tentative drafts were read and criticized. The authors wish to express their deep appreciation to the members of the Committee for their sympathetic and intelligent guidance of the project. In the final analysis, however, the authors themselves must take full responsibility for the complete text of the *Manual*.

The constant hope of the sponsoring Committee and the authors throughout the preparation of this *Manual* has been that it would be of service to institutions that want to take care of more students than are enrolled at present, without a corresponding increase in plant space. The *Manual* is directed particularly to the situation in institutions that do not have on their staffs some one who is already familiar with the techniques of gathering, analyzing, and interpreting the appropriate kinds of data for studies of plant space utilization. In this sense it is a "how to do it yourself" manual. The procedures are not so complicated but what they may be understood and applied by any institutional official. It is hoped that, by the use of agreed-upon definitions and standardized procedures, compilations of studies from many institutions can be made in the future in such a way as to provide more reliable norms of plant space utilization than are made available in this *Manual*.

The authors present this *Manual* with the hope that many institutions of higher education may be encouraged to undertake studies that will result in improving the efficiency of the utilization of their plant space.

JOHN DALE RUSSELL
JAMES I. DOI
Santa Fe, New Mexico, May 1957

Table of Contents

List of Tables

CHAPTER *1*

Functions and Limitations
of a College Space Utilization Study

A SPACE utilization study can be broadly defined as an organized procedure to obtain objective measures of the use made of space designed for a particular kind or kinds of activity. As an *organized* procedure, it is distinguished from an uncritical assembly of poorly defined data from which a meaningful interpretation cannot be produced. The need for emphasis on the *organized* nature of the procedure arises from observations of space utilization studies reported by institutions of higher education. A survey of such studies, recently completed in connection with the preparation of this *Manual*, indicates that oftentimes they are only haphazard collections of miscellaneous data from which no valid conclusions can be drawn. In a properly organized space utilization study, furthermore, the measures of use must be conceived and interpreted in terms of the particular kind of activity for which the space was designed. No single measure of utilization can be uncritically applied to all forms of space to determine the degree of use.

Why a Space Utilization Study?

The idea of a space utilization study is by no means new. Industry, business, governmental organizations, and the public schools have long ago developed well defined techniques of measuring space use and space needs. In the field of higher education, published reports of space utilization analysis that date back forty years or more can be found. The number of colleges and univer-

1

sities, however, that consistently make space utilization analyses in assessing building needs appears to be very small.

There are two compelling reasons why institutions of higher education should make space utilization studies. One is that knowledge of the degree and kind of use made of the physical plant is a condition of good management. The physical plant of a typical college or university represents a large investment of financial resources. It is costly to build, costly to maintain in good repair, and costly to heat, light, clean, and care for. Any addition to the physical plant should be made only after careful study indicates no space available within existing facilities to house adequately the services for which the addition is proposed.

There is a curious tendency in higher education to magnify the importance of the physical plant. A president oftentimes measures the success of his administration by the extent to which new buildings have been added to the campus since his inauguration. A department head takes enormous pride in having a new building constructed for his department, and in any large institution there is terrific competition among the various academic units as to which will get the next new building. Because other, less visible needs may be neglected in the glorification of plant facilities, it is desirable to check every proposal for plant expansion by a cold-blooded appraisal of needs based on a study of the utilization of existing facilities.

A second compelling reason for plant utilization studies is the prospect of large enrollment increases, dramatized by the now familiar phrase "the impending tidal wave of students." Authorities on higher education believe that, even by a very conservative estimate, the colleges and universities of the nation can expect a two-fold increase between 1956 and 1976, from approximately 3,000,000 students to 6,000,000. Some of the plant facilities needed to serve this greatly increased enrollment in the coming years will have to be provided through better utilization of available space.

There are two principal ways by which a college can accommodate more students. One is to enlarge the physical plant. The other is to make more effective use of existing facilities. These avenues are not mutually exclusive, and in actual practice, institutions of higher education will have to resort to both methods to meet the impending enrollment increases. Neither of these two routes will be easy.

The funds to finance new construction are not to be had just for asking. The current pressure for higher faculty salaries can be expected to grow more persistent; it is unquestionably the number one need in American higher education today. The prospective increases in enrollments will require more faculty members, additions to the administrative and library staffs, and more supplies and instructional materials. Funds for new construction will have to be raised and justified in the face of these inescapable pressures for greatly increased expenditures for current operating purposes.

Institutions that expect to participate in the task of caring for the impending enrollment increase cannot afford to ignore the possibility of making greater use of existing plant facilities. This may upset many established traditions governing the use of buildings, classrooms, laboratories, and office space. Many faculty members may feel inconvenienced. But more efficient use of building space, without reducing the quality of institutional programs, appears to be unavoidable in a period when colleges and universities are finding it increasingly difficult to obtain the funds needed to fulfill their obligations for instruction, research, and service.

The alternatives in caring for a rapidly expanding enrollment are by no means limited to an increase in plant facilities and an improvement in the utilization of space. One obvious course is for institutions to rearrange instructional programs so that a full-time student makes less use of institutional plant facilities than is customary at present. For example, many institutions require students to spend three hours in a science laboratory for one hour of credit, but others give an hour of credit for each two hours of laboratory exercise. At least one university has experimented with a program whereby the usual fifteen hours per week of attendance at lectures by a full-time student are condensed into nine or ten hours. Experimentation currently under way with television may reduce somewhat the need for classrooms of the conventional kind, enabling students to "attend" lectures in their dormitory rooms or at home. Rearrangements of instructional programs so as to require less use by the student of institutional plant facilities are beyond the scope of the present *Manual*. The concern in this *Manual* is with methods of studying and analyzing the utilization of plant space without regard to the kind of instructional program maintained.

Use Made of Space Utilization Data in Institutional Planning

The data resulting from space utilization analyses have been used by colleges and universities for three general purposes. Properly interpreted they have enabled institutions to make more effective use of existing plant space. The data frequently suggest the need for new patterns for scheduling classes and for new administrative devices for the control and assignment of classrooms and office space. It is not unusual for an institution to fall into a pattern of classroom use and office assignment that contributes to a feeling of crowdedness with the slightest increase in enrollments. A study of classroom utilization and office assignments may indicate, as it often does, that with a modification of the pattern the "overcrowded" situation can be corrected and many more students and staff members can be accommodated within existing facilities.

A comprehensive study of plant utilization has also proved to be a valuable technique for pinpointing specific building needs in conjunction with the development of a comprehensive program of plant expansion. The data, properly derived and interpreted, can help answer such questions as: What kinds of additional space are needed—laboratories, general classrooms, office space, library space, etc.? How much of each kind? What would be the most appropriate size of the new classrooms and laboratories? What kinds of offices are the most needed? An institution should not construct a building, however beautiful and pleasing to the eye, where none is needed; nor should it construct a building designed for a particular kind of use when a building of a different design suited for another purpose might better serve the needs of the institution. In order to avoid such unfortunate results, a space utilization study should be a necessary part of the planning for capital expansion.

Space utilization data have also come to be relied upon heavily by a number of state-supported institutions for the purpose of justifying requests for capital outlay appropriation and for establishing priorities among competing claims for needed buildings. Practically every college president sincerely believes his institution must have funds for capital outlay expansion and can put a convincing argument to support his claim. Few states, however, have sufficient funds to meet more than a fraction of the total amount requested for building purposes by all the state-supported colleges and universities. In the scramble that usually follows, the institution that has the most supporters in the legislature walks off with the lion's share of the available funds. On occasion legislative groups, in order to distribute funds for capital outlay on a more objective basis, resort to some formula for apportioning the total amount available, such as giving each institution an equal amount per student. Neither of these two methods for distributing capital outlay funds among competing institutions gives any assurance that the funds will be used for the most needed projects and where they would do the most good.

In a number of states today legislators and state fiscal authorities have come to realize that a uniform and coordinated space utilization study covering all the state-supported institutions is the best method so far devised for obtaining objective measures of capital outlay needs in a manner to afford comparison among competing claims for funds. It seems likely that church groups concerned with the support of two or more colleges might also resort to a similar device for assessing the relative building needs of their institutions of higher education. Individual donors, too, will probably come to insist on objective measures of building needs before loosening their purse strings.

Limitations of Space Utilization Data for Institutional Planning

The data from a study of space utilization consist primarily of mechanical and statistical measures of the physical plant. As such the data can form only the basis from which wise administrative decisions may be made regarding the best uses of the physical plant. Regardless of how well conceived a space utilization study may be, the resulting data should never be a substitute for experienced judgment. For example, on the basis of utilization data, a number of institutions of higher education have recently either voluntarily adopted or have been asked to adopt standards for use of classrooms and teaching laboratories. The standards, almost always higher than the existing rates of utilization, are usually stated in terms of numbers of hours or periods a week the facilities should be used. These standards are all products of judgment. The data on actual utilization may suggest that more efficient use can be made of existing facilities, but how much the rates of utilization might be increased without endangering the quality of the educational program is a matter of judgment.

Similarly, space utilization data are not, in and of themselves, solutions to problems arising out of the use and assignment of plant facilities. Such data can form the basis from which possible corrective courses of action may be instituted, but the pursuit of the solutions rests with an alert and intelligent administration.

Improvement in the percentage of utilization of space can be accomplished only through one or both of two basic procedures: (1) a reduction in the extent of plant space; (2) an increase in the number of students enrolled and in the extent to which they occupy plant facilities. Sometimes it is desirable, through a space utilization study, to show how rooms or buildings of poor quality, or space that is expensive to operate and maintain, can be abandoned. This is particularly applicable at present to a large number of campuses where rapidly deteriorating, temporary structures are still in use. More commonly, the objective of a utilization study is to determine how an increased enrollment may be accommodated without corresponding increase in floor space. Improvement in the utilization of plant space is not in and of itself a final goal. The goal is to save money that would otherwise be required for construction, operation, and maintenance of an over-extended plant, so that these funds may be used for other purposes that will contribute more to the achievement of the institution's fundamental aims and objectives.

While the plant is undeniably a facility which no modern college or university can do without or ignore in its planning, it is merely the stage for the performance of the institution's functions of instruction, research, and service. Plans for greater efficiency in the use of the physical plant should never be pushed in such a manner and to such a degree that the effectiveness and quality of the instructional, research, and service activities are impaired.

Scope of the Space Utilization Study

The purpose of a space utilization study determines to a large · extent the kinds of facilities to be studied and the nature of the analysis. The purpose may be identified by asking two questions: (1) What are the space problems? (2) What does the institution expect to do with the data after they are collected and analyzed?

If an institution feels pinched only for instructional space and does not feel crowded in other facilities, a study of space utilization limited to classrooms and laboratories would ordinarily be sufficient. If it is intended, however, to go a step further and find out approximately how many additional students might be accommodated in the present facilities, the study should include practically the entire plant. Classrooms and laboratories are but one kind of plant space affected by enrollment increases, and it would be a serious error to make estimates of the maximum potential capacity of a given plant on the basis of a study limited to only instructional space. Again, if the report is to be used primarily by institutional staff members as a guide to administrative actions on internal problems, the analyses should provide considerable detailed information. Classroom and laboratory utilization rates for departments, by course levels, and even by instructors might be computed. But if the institution intends to use the report primarily in support of a plea for funds to build additional facilities, the principal need is for summary data.

A clear understanding of the purpose of the plant utilization study will keep down the cost of the project by avoiding unnecessary work. A study encompassing the entire physical plant is a big job for most institutions. There is no need to undertake such a project if the space problems of the college can be successfully dealt with by a more modest study limited to certain special kinds of facilities.

Institutional Organization for a Space Utilization Survey

A space utilization study, unlike some other kinds of institutional surveys, does not require a team of outside experts. It can be done, as it most often is, by some member of the administrative staff or faculty, possibly with the guidance of other staff members. The registrar is usually in the best position to collect and organize the data for a space utilization study. On occasion an outside expert may advantageously be brought in to review the study, particularly if its recommendations have become or may become a subject of controversy within the institution.

A space utilization study should always be made by someone with an extensive educational background and with an educational point of view. It is not a job for a so-called efficiency expert who knows nothing of the problems of higher education.

The use of the institution's own staff members in a space utilization study has some very definite advantages. It encourages the institution to make such studies on a continuing basis as a regular feature of its program of internal analysis. Also the institution has a good guarantee that there may always be on hand a staff member or several staff members who are continually conscious of the need to make efficient use of plant space. One of the great disadvantages of surveys by outside experts is that practically everyone directly connected with the institution soon loses interest in the recommendations for change or forgets them entirely. An important advantage of the self-survey is that the institution can get the job done at less cost by using its own personnel than by bringing in outside experts.

The staff member or members who make the space utilization study need not be engineers or individuals familiar with the technical aspects of plant construction and management. It might be helpful to have a few such persons on a steering committee, but the selection of staff members for a committee to direct the study should be guided by the thought that many of their decisions will bear directly on the conduct of the instructional program. For example, it may be useful to include academic deans or other officers who will have to help put into practice the findings and recommendations of the space utilization study. The data under analysis will point toward such matters as scheduling of classes, class size, and classroom assignment. Many institutions that have organized space utilization studies under a committee have found it convenient to locate their center of operations in the office of the registrar.

CHAPTER 2

Current Status of
Space Utilization Studies

As A part of the project for the preparation of this *Manual*, an attempt was made to investigate the extent to which such studies have been made in recent years in the colleges and universities of the country. Two purposes were in mind in the attempt to collect copies of space utilization studies. The first was to see what the nature of these studies is as they are currently carried on, and to note what kinds of space were analyzed, what techniques were used, and what kind of conclusions were reached. The second purpose was to assemble data from space utilization studies from as large a number of institutions as possible, so as to provide tabulations that could be used as normative data. It was hoped that sufficient number of studies had been made on a comparable basis to permit the compilation of data into normative form.

In order to assemble studies of space utilization, the sponsoring Committee of the American Association of Collegiate Registrars, in the spring of 1956, sent an inquiry to each of its 1400 members, asking them to report any studies of this kind made in their institutions. Of the 961 who responded, only 241, or 25 per cent, indicated that a study of plant space utilization had been made for their institutions. Of the other 720 who indicated that no such study had been made recently, about 50 reported that it would be undertaken in the near future.

Each of the 241 respondents who indicated that a study has recently been made for his institution was asked to provide a copy of the report if it was available. Of this group, 65 were able to provide a copy or a summary of the results. Another 45 indicated that the data for their institutions were included in a published report prepared in connection with a state-wide survey of higher education. For the remaining 131 the Committee prepared a follow-up questionnaire asking for a summary of the results of the space utilization study. Slightly less than half of this group, 60, responded to the questionnaire, and about one-third of these indicated that the study was not actually a space utilization study as defined in the questionnaire form. A schedule of classroom assignment, involving practically no analysis of utilization, was frequently mistaken for a space utilization study. Subsequent examination of the copies and summaries of studies that were provided in answer to the request indicated that this limited conception of a space utilization study is not uncommon among college administrators.

By means of the inquiry sent to the members of the American Association of Collegiate Registrars and Admissions Officers and correspondence with directors of state-wide surveys of higher education, space utilization data pertaining to 223 institutions were obtained. Of this total, 129 institutions, or 55 per cent, were clearly identified as participants in various state-wide surveys of higher education. Practically all the data for these 223 institutions were for years since 1950.

Though the effort to obtain copies of space utilization studies was somewhat disappointing in the limited number of usable studies that could be found, it did yield some significant incidental information. For example, it was surprising to get replies from a number of registrars saying that no space utilization study had been made for their institution, when a copy of a report of a state-wide survey that included space utilization data for that institution was obtained from other sources. It appears also that the written report of a space utilization study made by an individual institution is generally not reproduced in quantity. Several institutions reported the existence of only two or three copies of their study, with circulation limited to certain administrative officials, and no copy available for use by anyone outside the institution.

A number of state-controlled institutions requested that the utilization data be treated as confidential, and if used in a published report that the institution not be identified by name. It seems that, in general, institutions prefer to maintain a certain degree of secrecy about information as to how their space is utilized. Sometimes, on reviewing the data, one would suspect that there is good reason for reticence about making the information public. A different attitude was noted among publicly controlled institutions that had recently been participants in a state-wide survey of higher education or that are located in states with a central coordinating agency; such institutions seemed to be the least concerned as to whether or not their space utilization data were kept confidential.

Table 1 shows the comprehensiveness of the plant studies obtained for the 223 institutions, with respect to the coverage of kinds of plant space. Instructional facilities were included in all 223 cases. For approximately three-fourths of the institutions, offices were also included. Other major kinds of plant space were included in many of the studies, but less frequently. Auxiliary facilities, such as dormitories, dining halls, and student union buildings, appear to be the most commonly omitted from plant studies. A comprehensive analysis of plant space is most likely to be made when institutions participate in a state-wide survey of higher education. An institution making its own study generally selects for examination only the kinds of plant space that are directly relevant to some special internal problem. Many institutions probably manage to cover the entire plant in a series of piecemeal studies, over a period of several years.

Instructional space was included in the studies for all 223 institutions. Most likely this reflects the fact that the inquiries for the plant utilization information had been addressed to a group of college administrators, the registrars, whose primary interest,

TABLE 1

Comprehensiveness of Physical Plant Studies for 223 Institutions of Higher Education

	TOTAL NUMBER OF STUDIES EXAMINED	NUMBER OF INSTITUTIONS INCLUDING FOLLOWING KINDS OF PLANT SPACE IN STUDY					
		Instructional Rooms	Offices	Libraries and Museums	Auditorium and Theatres	Gym and Field House	Auxiliary Activities
Institutions making own study for internal purposes	94	94	35	27	17	24	29
Institutions participating in state-wide surveys	129	129	129	129	129	129	46
TOTALS	223	223	164	156	146	153	75

TABLE 2

Comprehensiveness of Studies of Instructional Space for 223 Institutions

	TOTAL NUMBER OF STUDIES EXAMINED	NUMBER OF STUDIES IN WHICH FOLLOWING KINDS OF DATA WERE OBTAINED					
		Chart of Class Schedule or Inventory of Facilities Only, without Utilization Analysis	Utilization Analysis			Floor Area Related to Student-Stations or to Enrollment	Some Analysis Made of Quality of Facilities
			Room-Period Use Computed	Student-Station Use Computed	Differentiation Made of Kinds of Rooms		
Institutions making own study for internal purposes	94	27	66	44	61	20	18
Institutions participating in state-wide surveys	129	0	129	129	118	129	129
TOTALS	223	27	195	173	179	149	147

at least where plant facilities are concerned, is with instructional rooms. Had some other group of college officials, such as directors of libraries, also been covered by a similar inquiry, more studies pertaining to other plant facilities might have been obtained. Nonetheless, it would be appropriate to conclude that the major physical plant concern of institutions is with the availability of adequate instructional space for the anticipated increases in student enrollments.

Table 2 shows the comprehensiveness of the studies of instructional space for the 223 institutions. A total of 27, or 12 per cent, of the space utilization studies obtained turned out to be either a chart of classes scheduled or an inventory of facilities only, without any analysis of utilization. Data on classes scheduled and on the number of rooms used for instruction and the number of student stations contained in them are essential for a utilization analysis of instructional facilities, but unless related to show rates and patterns of use, such data do not constitute a study of utilization.

Some kind of measure of room-period use was computed for practically all of the institutions for which a utilization analysis of instructional space was made. Measures for both room-period use and student-station use were computed for all 129 institutions that were participants of state-wide surveys, but only two-thirds of the institutions making their own space utilization studies obtained both kinds of measures. In their analysis of instructional space, 179 institutions differentiated between various kinds of rooms, such as lecture rooms, teaching laboratories, etc. This is a decided departure from the practice of the pre-World War II era, when most space utilization studies made no distinction between the various kinds of instructional facilities.

For approximately two-thirds of the institutions, an effort was made in the studies to relate floor area either to the number of student stations or to student enrollment. The studies varied widely in the kinds of enrollment data used, thus rendering the results practically useless for purposes of comparison among institutions.

For about two-thirds of the institutions, the studies took into account the quality of plant facilities. By far the most common item of quality used in the studies was the permanency or non-permanency of the buildings. Only about one out of every ten institutions making a study of the quality of the instructional facilities attempted a systematic analysis of such items as seating arrangement, suitability of facilities for purpose used, adequacy of lighting, heating, ventilation, etc.

The general impression to be gained from an examination of available space utilization studies is that relatively few reports showed imaginative planning and skillful execution. For the most part they are limited with respect to the kinds of plant space included, limited in techniques of analysis, and generally lacking in interpretative material. It is clear that institutions have not had opportunity to use commonly understood definitions of terms in making such studies. The better studies made by individual institutions, as distinguished from those undertaken in connection with a state-wide survey, are generally for large universities that are staffed with one or more specialists who are particularly competent for making space utilization studies.

But a good space utilization analysis is not necessarily made only by a specialist. One of the most interesting and imaginative reports of space use and space needs found in this survey is for Marietta College, a small liberal arts college in Ohio. This report, entitled "A Study of Present Utilization of Physical Facilities, together with a Projection of Enrollment for 1960, 1965, 1970," was done by a staff member with no previous professional experience in making space utilization analyses for institutions of higher education.

Some of the space utilization studies made in connection with statewide surveys of higher education proved to be of disappointingly poor quality, though such surveys in general provided more examples of good studies than were found in any other source in this investigation. The "Restudy of the Needs of California in Higher Education," published by the California Department of Education in 1955, is notable for the scope and skillful execution of space analysis for a large group of institutions, including a large state university with several branches, a number of state colleges, private colleges and universities, and junior colleges. It is the best currently available source of standards for plant space needs in institutions with enrollments ranging from 2,000 to 25,000 full-time-equivalent students.

CHAPTER *3*

Definition of Terms

TERMS pertaining to measures of use and to the kinds of plant space should be defined. Following is a list of many of the common terms that occur in space utilization studies. The list is divided into two parts. The first part pertains to units and measures. The second part relates to categories of classification and kinds of plant space. Each term is briefly defined, and in some instances, an explanation is given as to its function in space utilization analysis. The concluding section of this chapter treats briefly the problem of defining quality of plant space.

Units and Measures Involved in Space Utilization Studies

1. *Class.*—An academic unit of one or more students formally organized for instruction in a specific course under the supervision of an instructor. A student or a group of students who may meet informally or irregularly for discussion with an instructor would not be considered a "class."

2. *Class meeting.*—A *regularly scheduled meeting* of one or more students assembled for instruction.

3. *Class size or size of class.*—The number of students enrolled in a class. The figure should include all who require accommodations in the place where the class meets, whether they are enrolled for credit, or as auditors. Normally the number appearing on the instructor's official class list as of the standard census date is considered the "size of the class."

Class size should be distinguished from course enrollments. Frequently they are one and the same. A course such as fresh-

17

man English composition, however, may have an enrollment of 300 students who are taught in 10 different sections. Each of these sections is a "class," and the number of students enrolled in a section constitutes its "size." In some institutions an instructor who teaches two or more sections of the same course submits only a single "class" list. Where this practice prevails, the data in the registrar's office should be referred back to the department chairman or to each faculty member for correction before they can be properly processed for a space utilization study.

A similar check should be made of data in the registrar's office in institutions where an instructor is permitted to teach two or more different courses at the same time and in the same room but submits a separate enrollment report for each course. This is particularly likely to occur in the departments of arts and crafts, music, and industrial arts. For a space utilization study, a group of students meeting in the same room and at the same time should be considered as a single class, irrespective of the courses in which they are enrolled.

4. *Period.*—As used in space utilization studies, a period is a unit of time approximating one hour. Generally in institutions of higher education a class period consists of 50 minutes of instruction, with an allowance of 10 minutes for changing classes. A class meeting scheduled for two consecutive hours, possibly a total of 110 minutes, should be considered as two class periods in a space utilization study. A class meeting scheduled for an hour and a half, which in most colleges would amount to 75 or 80 minutes of actual instruction, should be processed as 1.5 class periods in a space utilization study.

5. *Station.*—The total facilities necessary to accommodate one person at a given time. A *student station* is a chair, or a seat, or a laboratory desk, or some other facility necessary to accommodate one student during an instructional period. An *office station* generally consists of a desk and a chair and other office-type equipment required to accommodate one institutional staff member. A *research station* comprises the total laboratory-type facilities necessary to accommodate one research worker.

6. *Existing number of stations.*—The total stations contained in a room or a group of rooms at the time of the space inventory.

In making an inventory of existing stations, care must be taken to avoid duplication. Duplication is particularly likely to occur in classrooms if a count of movable kinds of student stations, such as unfixed chairs, is taken on separate days, or even at different hours of the same day if the building happens to be heavily used. The weekend or the student vacation period is the most appropriate time to take an inventory of existing student stations.

For certain kinds of facilities, such as a gymnasium playing floor or a shop-type laboratory, it will be necessary to make an estimate of the total number of students who can be accommodated at any one time. The advisable method here would be to ask the instructor or instructors who regularly hold classes in the room to determine the maximum number of students that can be comfortably accommodated for a class meeting.

7. *Optimum number of stations.*—The number of stations that can be practicably contained in a room or a group of rooms. There are two methods by which the optimum number of stations may be determined. One is to estimate the total number of people that can be comfortably accommodated at a given time by a proper layout of equipment in the room for the purpose for which it is being used. The other method is to divide the square feet of floor area of a room by some predetermined number of square feet of floor area for an individual station, the resulting quotient (to the nearest whole number) representing the total station capacity. This second method is difficult to apply in all instances because of the absence of reliable norms on the square feet of floor space per station required for each kind of room, such as administrative offices, faculty offices, general classrooms, physics laboratories, home economics laboratories, etc. Another difficulty is that the shape and the structural features of the room and the placement of heating devices and other equipment affect the number of stations that can be comfortably contained in a room.

8. *Weekly schedule.*—The days of the week and the hours during

which regularly scheduled classes are held. Institutions differ considerably in their weekly schedules, particularly with respect to the total number of hours. In space utilization studies, when dealing with rates of possible utilization, it is essential to identify the number of hours on a weekly basis that has been used to compute the rates. For the most part, the rates of possible utilization referred to in this *Manual* are computed on the basis of a weekly schedule of a given number of hours.

The weekly schedule has been selected for the purposes of this discussion because it is the most frequently used in space utilization studies. This should not, however, obscure the fact that it may be advantageous to compute rates of utilization on an annual rather than on a weekly basis. Such measures may suggest revisions in institutional schedules that would permit more efficient use of physical facilities over a 12-month period.

9. *Square feet of floor space.*—A common unit of measure encountered in space utilization studies is the square foot of floor area. Data on square feet of floor space are obtained for the purpose of relating floor area to a given unit, such as a department of instruction, or a full-time-equivalent student, or a faculty member. Cubic footage is rarely used in space utilization studies.

In describing the floor area of a building, it is suggested that a distinction be made among *gross space, inside gross* or total interior, and *assignable space*.

(a) *Gross space* is the over-all square feet measurement of a building, including the area taken up by structural elements such as exterior and interior walls and columns.

(b) *Inside gross space* is the square feet of area in the interior of a building, excluding structural elements such as walls and columns.

(c) *Assignable space* excludes from the *inside gross* measurement all floor area used for janitorial and building maintenance services, public washrooms, unfinished rooms, and general circulation areas, such as corridors, stairways, and elevators.

In obtaining the assignable floor area for a room, such as a classroom, a laboratory, or an office, it is customary to measure between the principal surfaces of the walls and partitions at or near the floor level. Space occupied by alcoves, closets, and built-in shelves opening into and serving the room should ordinarily be included in the count of total assignable square feet of floor space. For ease in obtaining measurements, area of columns, door-swings, and impaired headroom, and space occupied by heating devices may be ignored; if, however, any of these structural features constitutes a large loss of usable space, the area should be deducted from the square feet measurement of the room.

10. *Measures of utilization.*—Measures of utilization of instructional space generally have as their basis one of two units, the room and the student station. Following are the commonly used measures of utilization relating to these two units:

(a) *Room-period use* is the number of hours that a room (or the average for a group of rooms) is occupied by a class. A room is considered to be in use whenever a class meeting is held in it, regardless of the size of the class.

(b) The room-period use may be expressed as the percentage of possible periods during the day or the week that a room or a group of rooms is occupied by a class. The resulting measure should be referred to as the *percentage of room-period use*. For example, if an institution operates its schedule on a 44-hour week and has a total of 50 instructional rooms, it has a total of 2,200 possible room periods. If during the week a total of 1,100 class meetings are scheduled in these rooms, the average "room-period use" would be 22 hours. The "percentage of room-period use" on a weekly basis would be 50.

(c) *Student-station-period use* is the number of hours that student stations are occupied. For example, if during the week a room is occupied for 22 room periods by classes averaging 45 students each, its student-station-period use for the week would be 990. By itself the figure on student-station-period use is not very meaningful. It should therefore be related to either the number of existing student stations or the number of possible student-station periods.

(d) The relationship between student-station-period use and the number of existing student stations may be expressed as the average number of *student hours per station*. Thus, for a 60-student-station room with a weekly student-station-period use of 990, the "student hours per week per station" would be 16.5.

(e) The student-station-period use may also be expressed as the percentage of possible periods during the week (or a given hour or a given day) that student-stations are occupied. For example, on a 44-hour weekly schedule a room containing 60 student stations would have a total of 2,640 possible student-station periods. If during the week this group of student stations is occupied for a total of 990 periods, the *percentage of possible student-station-period use* for the room would be 37.5. It should be noted that the average student hours per station discussed in the preceding paragraph can be easily converted to the percentage of possible student-station-period use by dividing it by the institution's weekly schedule. The formula is:

$$\left(\frac{\text{average student hours per station}}{\text{weekly schedule}}\right) 100 = \begin{array}{l}\text{percentage of possible} \\ \text{student-station-period use}\end{array}$$

(f) Another measure of student-station use is the *utilization of student stations in occupied rooms*. It is the average percentage of student stations occupied in classrooms when the classrooms are actually in use. Care should be exercised not to confuse this measure with that defined in the preceding paragraph as the "percentage of student-station-period use."

(g) A somewhat different measure of utilization, from those which have as their basis either the room or the student station, is the "square feet of assignable instructional floor space per 100 hours of student occupancy per week." This measure makes possible a comparison among institutions of the relationship of floor space to student usage, without regard to institutional variations in the average square feet of area allotted per student station. One hundred hours of student occupancy is being suggested as the unit, although a larger or a smaller number of hours can be selected as the unit of measure for this relationship.

Categories for Classification of Plant Space

It is important in studies of plant space utilization to classify building areas on the basis of their primary use or function. The various kinds of plant space and the definition of each are as follows.

1. *Academic space.*—All space assigned for use by academic units, including that used for classrooms and teaching laboratories, offices, faculty research, storage of academic equipment and supplies, and conferences.

2. *Instructional space.*—Any room scheduled for class meetings. Some institutions, in making space utilization studies, use this term to include all space assigned to the academic units. It is suggested that "instructional space" be reserved to designate only such space as is regularly used for class meetings.

A room regularly used for or available for class meetings should be classified as "instructional space" regardless of the designation of the building in which it is located. On many campuses, instructional rooms are found in the "administration building," or the "library building," or the "field house," or the "student union building."

Following are descriptions of the major kinds of instructional space found in institutions of higher education:

(a) A *general classroom* is an instructional room used chiefly for lectures, recitation, and seminar type of class meetings. Other common terms for this are "non-specialized instructional space" and "lecture room."

On occasions, in space utilization studies, differentiation is made between general classrooms and seminar rooms. In such instances a seminar room is identified as an instructional room equipped with a large table and chairs, and the general classroom as an instructional room equipped with only seating for student use and a desk, table, or lectern and chair for the instructor.

"General classrooms" are sometimes furnished with special equipment to serve the needs of a particular subject. For example, rooms used by classes in history may have wall maps, classrooms for mathematics may have extra blackboards, classrooms for foreign languages may have recording and record-playing equipment, etc. A room should be classified as a "general classroom," if it is designed for lecture and recitation-type class meetings and if its equipment does not render it unsuitable for use by classes in almost any subject.

(b) A *teaching laboratory* is an instructional room equipped for a special purpose such as chemistry experiments, food preparation and service in home economics, shop-work in industrial arts, painting, etc. Adjoining space, such as a balance room, storeroom, supply room, dark room, or projection room, should be classified as "teaching laboratory service area." A teaching laboratory should be distinguished from a research laboratory that is not ordinarily made available for class meetings.

Certain specialized rooms, such as those set up for instruction in business machines and accounting, drafting, sewing, biology, and band practice, can generally be used also for lecture and recitation-type class meetings. Notwithstanding this flexibility of usage, these rooms should be classified as teaching laboratories. They are equipped primarily for a specialized, laboratory-type instructional activity, and not for lecture and recitation-type classes.

Teaching laboratories designed for different activities are seldom exactly alike with respect to the square feet of floor space required for a student station or with respect to rates of utilization. Thus, an institution will generally find it advisable to make a detailed analysis of laboratories according to the special functions, subjects, and levels of instruction for which they were designed.

(c) A *music practice room* is instructional space used by a student for the individual practice of some musical instrument. It may be classified as a special kind of teaching laboratory, but it is generally advisable to make a separate analysis of the utilization of this kind of room. Another kind of special teaching laboratory similar to the music practice room is the *music studio*. The music studio is generally larger than the music practice room and is designed to accommodate several persons at one time. A music studio assigned to a faculty member which serves as a combination faculty office and music studio, should be classified as a faculty office.

(d) *Playing floors, wrestling and boxing rooms, indoor swimming pools*, and *indoor track and field areas*, housed in the gymnasium or field house, constitute special types of instructional space. Spectator seating areas, locker and shower rooms, and equipment issue and storage rooms located in the gymnasium should be classified as "gym service area." The *seating area of an auditorium or theatre*, if regularly used for scheduled class meetings, should be classified as a general purpose lecture room.

3. *Office.*—A room or a suite of rooms with office-type equipment that is assigned to one or more staff members for the performance of administrative, clerical, or faculty duties other than meeting of classes. Waiting rooms, office files and supply rooms, interconnecting corridors within a suite of offices, private toilets, and clothes closets should be classified as "office service area." A studio room in the department of music or fine arts, assigned to one or more faculty members for their own work, even though occasionally used for a student lesson, should be classified as a faculty office.

4. *Conference room.*—A room generally equipped with a large table and chairs, to which classes or staff members are not regularly assigned.

5. *Research laboratory.*—A special purpose room that provides research facilities and is not made available for regular class meetings. A room that serves both as an office and a research laboratory should be classified as a research laboratory. Institutions having programs of contract or sponsored research should classify space used for this purpose separately from that used for research

carried on under the regular institutional budget. This is necessary if proper charges are to be made against the research contract for plant overhead.

6. *Library space.*—A room or a group of rooms used for the collection, storage, circulation, and use of books, periodicals, manuscripts, and other reading and reference materials. This category should include the general library, departmental libraries, and rooms for special collections of documents, films, or records. Library science laboratories and lecture classrooms located in the library building should be classified as instructional rooms, and should be excluded from the inventory of "library space." Following are definitions for some special kinds of library space:

(a) *Stacks*, shelving located within a library for the housing of books, periodicals, and manuscripts. Similar facilities located in conference rooms, offices, and classrooms should not be classified as "stack space";

(b) *Carrell*, an individual study station within or adjoining the stacks;

(c) *Reading room* (or study hall), space in the library equipped with tables and chairs for reading and study; browsing room should be included as a part of the reading room area.

(d) *Periodical room*, a room used for the collection, display, and reading of current periodicals, often equipped also with tables and chairs;

(e) *Library service area*, space designated for the processing and circulation of library material such as acquisitions room, cataloguing room, document reproduction room, circulation and reference desks.

In addition to the foregoing kinds of space, which will be found in practically every college library, some libraries have rooms set aside for film review, rare book collections, and listening booths for records and tape recordings. All such rooms should come under the category of "library space."

7. *Museum* or *exhibition room.*—Any room used for display of special collections, such as historical documents, mineral samples,

stuffed animals, fossils, etc. Rooms used for preparation of exhibits or storage of exhibits should be designated as "museum service areas."

8. *Auditorium and theatre.*—Any room possessing a stage, audience seating, and other equipment for the purpose of presenting dramatic plays, concerts, and similar events. As previously indicated, if the seating area is regularly used for scheduled class meetings, it can be classified as a special type of instructional space.

Check rooms, ticket sales booths, dressing rooms, projection room, scenery room, etc., should be placed under the general category of "auditorium (or theatre) service area."

9. *Armory.*—Indoor drill areas should be treated as a special kind of instructional space, similar to gymnasium playing floors, and differentiated from space classifiable as "general classrooms" or "teaching laboratories." Uniform and equipment storage and issue room should be placed in the general category of "armory service area."

10. *Animal quarters.*—Space used for the housing and feeding of animals. It is suggested that quarters for such small animals as rats and guinea pigs, located in academic buildings, be analyzed separately from buildings designated as barns and stables.

11. *Greenhouse.*—A room or a building used for the protection and cultivation of plants.

12. *Student living, recreational, and non-instructional service areas.*—All space used for student and staff living, recreation and services ancillary to the instructional and research functions of the institution. Following are the kinds of rooms and service units that fall in this broad category:

(a) *Chapel*, a room designated for devotional activities. Choir dressing rooms, organ loft, etc., should be designated as "chapel service area."

(b) *Cafeteria and dining hall*, any room or group of rooms equipped with tables and chairs or counters and stools and used for serving of regular meals. Kitchens, serving areas, and food storage rooms should be designated as "cafeteria (or dining hall) service area." Snack bars and soda fountains, except where maintained as an integral part of a cafeteria or dining hall, should be classified as merchandising service areas. (See below.)

(c) *Residence hall,* any group of rooms designated as living quarters for students. These facilities may include some space for one or more faculty members who serve as counsellors in the residence hall.

(d) *Student union (including faculty clubs),* all enclosed space such as lounges, smoking rooms, game rooms, bowling alleys, etc., designated for student and staff recreation and rest.

(e) *Merchandising service areas,* category for the inclusion of space used for snack bar, soda fountain, barbershop, book exchange, and bookstore. Similar facilities located off the campus and in buildings not owned and operated by the institution should not be included.

(f) *Health clinic and infirmaries,* building or room designated for student health service. All space used for this service, such as examination rooms, treatment rooms, sick beds, etc., should be included in this category.

(g) *Faculty housing.* It is suggested that plant units devoted exclusively to housing of faculty be excluded from the analysis of utilization of space.

13. *Accessory space.*—A general category for the inclusion of all rooms and areas within a building existing for the convenience of all who use the building, such as corridors, lobbies, stairwells, elevators, and public rest rooms and for the maintenance and servicing of the building, such as janitorial closets, furnace room, and boiler room. Corridors, lobbies, stairwells, and elevators may be grouped under the sub-category "circulatory space," and janitorial closets and furnace and boiler rooms as "custodial space"; public rest rooms should be a separate sub-category.

14. *Buildings and grounds service space.*—A general category for all workshops for buildings and grounds and storage units that serve the entire campus. Examples are the storage warehouses

for items of general supply and equipment, garage and automotive service buildings, work rooms for painting, carpentry, electrical repairs, plumbing, machine repair and maintenance, and the central heating plant. Each of these facilities may be classified under one of two sub-groupings—"Shop" and "Storage."

15. *Inactive space.*—A category for the inclusion of all rooms that are not in use at the time of the space utilization study, because of new construction, major alteration, or condemnation. For the purposes of a space utilization study, note should be made of the number of different kinds of inactive rooms and the square feet of floor space involved, but such data should be clearly distinguished from those reported for space that is in use or is available for use.

Quality of Space

In making studies of utilization of plant space it is helpful to classify floor areas in accordance with the quality of the space. Not infrequently, space of poor quality in a temporary building is found to be used more heavily than excellent space in a permanent building. The determination of the quality of a given plant facility is necessarily subjective. Quality ratings can be given with reasonable accuracy and reliability by an experienced person upon an examination of the various rooms and other plant facilities.

Quality, as it pertains to a building, is primarily a question of the general state of usefulness. Is it permanent or temporary? Can it be continued in use indefinitely with only ordinary maintenance, or will it require considerable alterations and improvements? Quality, as it pertains to a room within a building, usually involves the general appearance of the room and its suitability for the purpose for which it is used. Characteristics useful in analyzing the quality of a building or a room are outlined in a later chapter concerned with procedure and forms for the collection of data.

CHAPTER *4*

Forms and Procedure
for the Collection of Data

A SUITABLE set of forms for the collection of data is an important tool of a space utilization study. The number of forms needed and the design for each depend upon the scope and purpose of the survey. The set of forms for the collection of data suggested in this *Manual*, if used in its entirety, would result in a fairly comprehensive survey of college plant facilities. An institution wishing to make a study limited to one or two kinds of plant space should select only the forms pertaining to those facilities.

Instructional Rooms

Of utmost importance in a utilization study of instructional facilities is the identification of all instructional rooms known to exist on the campus. One of the first tasks in making a space utilization study is to prepare an accurate, up-to-date inventory of all available instructional rooms, if such a record does not already exist.

The inventory record should preferably be in the form of a card file, with a card for each instructional room. This will facilitate certain kinds of space utilization analysis, for the cards can be readily arranged into various desired groupings and the data tabulated directly from them. Also a card file inventory, once established, can be kept up to date by inserting a new card for each additional room resulting from new construction and by removing a card for each room that ceases to exist because of extensive remodeling or razing of old buildings. Institutions that intend to make space utilization studies on a continuing basis will find a card file inventory of instructional rooms particularly valuable.

Form 1 suggests the design for an instructional room inventory card. Each instructional room should be identified by building name or code and by room number. The appropriate information on number of student stations, principal use of room, de-

FORM 1

Inventory of Instructional Rooms

Building _____ Room number _____ Number of student stations _____

Principal use of room _____

Department controlling room _____

Notes: Date Recorded   By

Assignable floor area:

(a) Total square feet _____ (b) Square feet per student station _____

partment controlling room (if any), total assignable square feet, and assignable square feet per student station should be entered. Space is also provided on Form 1 for the entry of special notes relevant to the information items listed. In setting up its system of inventory cards an institution may want to use a color scheme for ready identification of certain characteristics of rooms, such as their principal use.

Form 1 calls for the existing number of student stations, rather than the optimum number (see chapter III, page 19, for distinction), because the existing number is generally the easier of the two inventory figures to obtain. The optimum number of student stations, when obtained, is usually in addition to and for the purpose of rendering comparison with the existing number. Form 1 can be readily modified to include both of these inventory figures, if an institution wishes to make this comparative analysis.

"Principal use of room" should indicate whether it is a general lecture room, or some kind of teaching laboratory, such as a physics laboratory, a home economics sewing room, or a drafting room. If gymnasium playing floors and auditorium seating areas are to be included in the analysis as special kinds of instructional rooms, they should be appropriately described so there will be no mistaking their identity.

The name of the department or administrative agency controlling the use of the room, if any, should be entered in the blank "Department Controlling Room." Some institutions have the policy of assigning each room to a department and the use of that room thereafter is controlled by the department, whether it is the sole user or not. In other institutions, a central administrative agency, such as the registrar's office, controls the use of instructional rooms, and no one academic department can lay claim to a classroom. Central administration of the assignment of use of rooms nearly always results in a more effective utilization of space than the policy of allocating rooms to particular departments that control the use of such space.

The next step, after completing the inventory file for instructional rooms, is the preparation of a class-schedule report. Form 2 suggests the data to be included in this report. A Form 2 should be completed for each class taught on the campus during the term or semester of the year selected for the space utilization study. The necessary data are ordinarily on file in the registrar's office. If that office has any doubts of the accuracy of the formal class records, each Form 2 should be referred to the appropriate department head for confirmation and correction.

It is important to note that the unit under consideration in

Form 2 is the *class* and not the *course*. Class enrollment and course enrollment are frequently the same, but a course may be taught in several different sections, each of which comprises a separate class. Also students enrolled in two or more different courses may be taught as a single class by the same instructor at the same time and place. In this latter case, the entries for course data should

FORM 2
Class-Schedule Report

Term and year _____ Department _____

A. Course data   B. Class data

Course & section number _____   Class (section) enrollment _____

Course level _____   Type of instruction _____

                            Building & room _____

C. Notes:

D. Chart of class-meeting schedule

INDICATE HOUR OF DAY	ENTER CLASS (SECTION) ENROLLMENT					
	Monday	Tuesday	Wednesday	Thursday	Friday	Saturday

reflect the two or more different courses that are taught as a single class. The primary purpose of the course data in Form 2 is to identify the class.

"Department" in Form 2 refers to the academic unit sponsoring the course, and not to the department controlling the instructional space. The class should be identified by course and section number, if the course is taught in more than one section. "Course level" should indicate the academic level of instruction, such as "freshman" (Fr), "sophomore" (So), "junior" (Jr), "senior" (Sr), or "graduate" (Grad). The letters in parentheses are suggested abbreviations for the various academic levels. "Class (section) enrollment" should show the number of students enrolled in the class. "Type of instruction" should indicate whether the class is "non-laboratory," "laboratory," or "others." More specific designations of the type of instruction may be used if desired, but for most purposes of space utilization analysis, the three broad categories are usually sufficient. "Building and room" should clearly indicate the place of the class meetings. Building and room designations should in all instances coincide with those used in the inventory record of instructional rooms. For example, if the building used for science instruction is popularly known as "Old Main," do not use "Old Main" on one form and "Science" on another to identify the same building. In reporting the hours of the class meetings, care should be taken to show both the beginning and the terminating hours of the class meetings. For example, if the class begins at 9:00 A.M. and ends at 10:00 A.M., the proper entry for the hours of the day should be "9–10 A.M.," and not merely "9:00 A.M." If a class meets for two consecutive hours, for example from 9–11:00 A.M., there should be two entries for hours of the day, one reading "9–10:00 A.M." and the other "10–11:00 A.M." Also if a class meets at different hours on different days, the entries for days and hours should accurately reflect this situation. If a class is scheduled to meet in different rooms during the week, a separate Form 2 should be made for each meeting place. Appropriate comment of this special feature should be made in the section for "Notes," including a cross-reference to other Form 2's pertaining to the same class.

A Form 2 should be prepared for each class that meets on an "arranged" basis, even though the time and place of meeting are not regularly scheduled and therefore cannot be readily identified. The data for "arranged" classes cannot be incorporated into the analysis of instructional space use in the same way as for the regularly scheduled classes, but an estimate should be made of the student contact hours involved and the data shown in the written report to indicate the extent of such class activity.

On occasion an institution may have an accelerated class, one that does not run the full length of the term or semester, or a class that meets on alternate weeks. Such special features of class meetings should be carefully noted in the space provided for "Notes." The suggested method for processing data for accelerated classes and classes that meet on alternating weeks is to restrict the utilization analysis only to classes that meet on a given week of the term or semester selected for the study. The fourth or fifth week after the start of the term (except possibly for the summer session) would be a good week to choose, for by then the class lists would have been completed by the registrar and sent back to the instructors. Any class that was not scheduled to meet during the week chosen should be omitted from the space utilization analysis.

Forms 1 and 2, when completed, will provide all the basic data necessary for most of the usual kinds of utilization analyses made of instructional rooms. To be most valuable for institutional purposes, the data in Form 2 should be collected and subjected to analysis at regular intervals, preferably once every year or two years for the semester or term that normally represents the institution's peak load. The exact frequency interval for repeating the study would be dependent on such factors as rate of enrollment change and additions to the plant.

Form 3 is for the collection of data on the quality of accommodations in instructional rooms. These data might well be part of a comprehensive study of instructional space that might be made at intervals of every three or five years. The analysis of quality of space, however, should be optional and can be omitted if there are no issues on which such information would be helpful. The upper part of Form 3 can be completed from data collected in Form 1, the inventory card for each instructional room. The lower part of the form, the items pertaining to quality, will require the examiner or a team of examiners to inspect each instructional room. If several persons are to do the rating, each taking a different group of rooms, it is suggested that they first inspect a number of rooms together and attempt to work out a set of criteria so each can rate the rooms on a nearly comparable basis. The examiner should make liberal use of the space reserved for notes and comments, for he will find them most valuable later for a review or explanation of his ratings.

Following are some points and room characteristics that an examiner might keep in mind as he rates each room:

1. *Relation of number of student stations to floor area:* A general lecture classroom with fixed, unmovable student stations would normally be rated as either "space tightly used but adequate" or "comfortable amount of space," unless some very poor planning occurred during the construction process. Regardless of the size of the room there should be enough space in the aisle and between each student station to allow students to file in and out of the room without having to move the chairs and bump into them. Each seat should be so spaced that a student can write and occasionally shift his position without jostling the person next to him. A room should not be so packed with student stations that some students will have to sit practically touching radiators, windows, or chalkboards. In every lecture or demonstration-type room there should be ample space in front for an instructor to move about freely during the course of his lecture.

The square feet of floor space per student station is not a sure guide as to the sufficiency of space in an instructional room. Variations in size and shape of a classroom can cause wide differences in the square feet of floor space per student station. Some rooms, particularly teaching laboratories, have exhibit cabinets, display tables, and supply cabinets that take up considerable floor space. Other rooms may have pillars or bulky heating devices which tend to reduce the number of student stations that can be comfortably accommodated.

All these factors and others that may come to the attention of the examiner as he inspects an instructional room should be

Name of institution ───────────────────

FORM 3

Quality of Accommodations in Classroom or Laboratory or Other Room for Instructional Purposes

(one page for each room)

Building ─────── Room number ─── Number of student stations ───

Assignable sq. feet of floor area ─────── Assignable sq. feet of floor area per

student station ───────.

Department controlling use of room ─────────────────

Principal use of room ───────────────────────

Other uses that can be made of room ─────────────────

The items below are to be filled out by examiner at time of his visit.

1. Relation of number of student stations to floor area
   ─── a. Overcrowded room
   ─── b. Space tightly used but adequate
   ─── c. Comfortable amount of space
   ─── d. More space than necessary

2. Quality of accommodations for principal purposes
   ─── a. Excellent
   ─── b. Satisfactory
   ─── c. Poor
   ─── d. Very deficient

3. General impression of the room
   ─── a. Pleasant and attractive
   ─── b. Satisfactory
   ─── c. Dreary and unattractive

4. Specific deficiencies noted:
   ─── a. Shape of room
   ─── b. Placement of windows
   ─── c. Artificial light
   ─── d. Heating
   ─── e. Ventilation
   ─── f. Seating
   ─── g. Instructor's desk
   ─── h. Instructional equipment
   ─── i. Chalkboard
   ─── j. Bulletin board
   ─── k. Walls and ceiling
   ─── l. Floor
   ─── m. Decoration
   ─── n. Acoustics
   ─── o. External noise
   ─── p. Other (specify)

Special notes or comments:

─────────────   ─────────────
Examiner   Date

taken into account in determining the qualitative relationship of number of student stations to the floor area.

2. *Quality of accommodations for principal purposes:* This is essentially a question of the general state or condition of the equipment in the room. If the chairs, tables, or laboratory desks look as if they have been much used and abused and are badly in need of repair or replacement, the room should be rated as either poor or deficient. Laboratory desks inadequately equipped for modern instructional programs would bring down the rating of the room. The condition of the chalkboard, window shades, fixtures, the instructor's desk, should all be taken into consideration.

3. *General impression of the room:* This should be an attempt to rate the room itself, without regard to quality of the equipment housed in the room. Stained walls and ceiling, cracked plaster, poorly maintained overhanging plumbing fixtures and heating ducts, cracked windowpanes, and damaged or excessively worn flooring tend to detract from the pleasantness and attractiveness of a room.

4. *Specific deficiencies noted:* Many of the items listed in this short check list of room features should have been taken into consideration in rating the quality of accommodations for principal purposes and the general impressions of the room. An "x" mark should be placed in the blank in front of the item that is judged to be deficient in some respect. This list is useful chiefly for the plant maintenance department as an indication of specific points that need attention.

A room that is long and narrow or broken up by columns or pillars should be considered improperly shaped. Adequate lighting is a necessary attribute of a good classroom and deserves special attention. Natural light is a desirable feature for most classrooms, but even more important is good artificial lighting. Windows should be placed so that neither any student nor the instructor has to face a source of outside light.

Adequacy of heating, so far as Form 3 is concerned, is basically a question of whether a room is equipped with heating facilities or

not. On occasion in an old building that has been partially remodeled, there is a room or two without proper heating. Ventilation is especially important in chemistry laboratories, and such
rooms should be examined for fume hoods and exhaust fans.
Basement rooms frequently tend to be poorly ventilated and
should be carefully inspected for adequacy of ventilation.

Seating, as used here, refers to both the seating arrangement
and to the quality of the seating, but not to the relationship of
number of student stations to the floor area. Student-stations
should be arranged so that the natural light from windows falls
to the left of the right-handed students. The seating should be
comfortable and should provide adequate space for note taking
and the writing of examinations.

Each classroom should ordinarily be equipped with a chair and
a desk or a table for the instructor. A podium or lectern may in
some instances adequately substitute for a desk. Lack of such
facility for the instructor should be considered a specific deficiency. The requirements for instructional equipment vary
from one room to another, depending on the principal use of the
room. It is suggested that the examiner attempt to familiarize
himself with the kinds of instructional equipment considered
essential to rooms of each kind before visiting the rooms. In the
cases of both the instructor's desk and instructional equipment,
quality or condition should also be taken into consideration.
Equipment badly in need of repair or replacement should be re-
garded as a specific deficiency.

Practically every instructional room (except gymnasium playing floors, auditoriums, and other special kinds of instructional
space) should have, as a part of its equipment, a chalkboard. The
chalkboard should be examined for bad cracks, discoloration,
pits, and similar defects. A classroom bulletin board is an item
that many students and instructors find very useful. In a modern
instructional room lack of a bulletin board is almost as serious a
deficiency as lack of a chalkboard.

As indicated earlier, the walls, ceiling, and floor of a room should be inspected. Large cracks and water marks on the walls and ceiling, and splintered and excessively worn flooring should be noted. The walls, if painted, should appear fresh and unsoiled. Decoration, such as pictures on the wall, help to make a sometimes drab classroom more pleasant.

Acoustics is an important element of a classroom and an attempt should be made to determine its quality. An easy method for determining the acoustical quality of a room is to check with instructors who have used the room. If there are serious defects, they would be the most likely to know. Similarly external noise is another factor that can be easily determined by checking with faculty members who have used the room. External noise is frequently a disturbing element in classroom buildings located near machine shops, voice and instrumental music rooms, highways, airports, and playing fields.

This brief description of what to look for in the way of specific deficiencies in instructional rooms is by no means exhaustive. A complete discussion of specific room deficiencies is beyond the scope of this *Manual*. A detailed discussion of the requirements for various kinds of instructional rooms may be found in Evenden, Strayer, and Engelhardt's *Standards for College Buildings*. This book was published in 1938, and may be out of date for certain kinds of laboratory facilities.

Offices, Research Laboratories, and Conference Rooms

Form 4 is for the collection of data for offices and research laboratories. A form should be filled out for each room used for any one or both of these purposes. Music and fine arts studios, if they serve as offices, should be included. Partitioned areas within a large room should be processed as individual rooms.

With minor changes Form 4 can be adapted for inventory of waiting rooms and conference rooms. "Total number of person-stations in room" can be changed to read "total seating capacity of room." For those using the room, only the department or administrative unit need be shown.

Name of institution _____

FORM 4

Faculty and Administrative Offices and Research Laboratories

(one page for each room used for office or laboratory of one or more staff members)

Building _____ Room number _____ Assignable sq. feet of floor area _____

Total number of person-stations in room _____ Assignable sq. feet of floor area

per station _____

Use made of room: (check one) Office _____; Laboratory (or studio) _____; or

Combination office and laboratory (or studio) _____

List below those using the room:

NAMES OF STAFF MEMBERS ASSIGNED TO ROOM	DEPARTMENT OR ADMINISTRATIVE UNIT (IF ROOM USED FOR DUTIES OF SEVERAL DEPARTMENTS, SO INDICATE.)	RANK OR TITLE OF STAFF MEMBERS

Indicate below the kind and amount of equipment ordinarily maintained in room.

EQUIPMENT ITEM	NUM-BER	QUALITY			EQUIPMENT ITEM	NUM-BER	QUALITY		
		Exc.	Ave.	Poor			Exc.	Ave.	Poor
Desks					Bookshelves (no. of lineal ft.)				
Chairs					Filing cases (no. of drawers)				
Tables					Telephones				
Cabinets					Typewriters				
Wastebaskets					Typewriter stands or tables				

Other (Specify on back of this page.)

The check-list below is to be filled out by the examiner at time of visit to room.

QUALITY			ITEM
Exc.	Ave.	Poor	
			1. Adequacy of space for number assigned
			2. Provisions for privacy
			3. General attractiveness of room
			4. Quality of accommodations (over-all impression)
			5. Adequacy of lighting
			6. Other comments:

_____   _____
Examiner   Date

41

Except for the quality ratings, which should be made by the examiner, Form 4 can, if necessary, be completed by a clerk or secretary of the administrative unit or instructional department. A covering letter of instructions, particularly with respect to such matters as how to compute the assignable square feet of floor area, will help reduce to a minimum errors and discrepancies. This piecemeal approach, however, does have its hazards. For the most uniform results, the examiner himself should make these measurements.

The procedure for rating the quality of rooms used for offices and staff research laboratories is much the same as that previously described for instructional rooms. The examiner should bear in mind that adequacy of space for the number of persons assigned to an office and the need for privacy vary from one office to another, depending on the duties of the occupant or occupants. Administrative officers, such as presidents and deans, require more space and better provisions for privacy than members of the clerical staff or faculty members. A comprehensive discussion of the specific needs of various offices may be found in Evenden, Strayer, and Engelhardt's *Standards for College Buildings*.

Service Areas for Instructional Rooms, Offices, and Research Laboratories

Form 5 is for the collection of data for service areas for instructional rooms, offices, and research laboratories. Most teaching and research laboratories are served by separate rooms designated for the storage of supplies and special equipment and the preparation of teaching and research aids. Lecture rooms are sometimes equipped with projection booths for the use of films and slides. Clerical and administrative offices are usually served by file rooms, supply storage rooms, and mimeograph rooms. Each such room should be identified and separately reported in Form 5. Animal rooms and greenhouses should also be processed by this form, if their usage indicates that they can be classified as instructional or research laboratory service space. The "principal use of room" and "department, office, and other unit controlling room" should be clearly designated so that each room may be classified as either instructional service, office service, or research laboratory service.

Name of institution

FORM 5

Service Rooms for Instructional Purposes, Offices, and Research Laboratories

(one page for each room)

Building _____ Room number _____ If no number, designate location

by indicating numbered room or rooms leading into it _____

Principal use of room _____

Department, office, or other unit controlling room _____

Assignable square feet of floor area _____

Notes on quality of facilities for purpose used:

Examiner _____ Date _____

Libraries, Auditoriums, and Gymnasiums

Forms 6, 7, and 8 are for the collection of data for libraries, auditoriums (and theatres and assembly halls), and gymnasiums (and field house and armory), respectively. In each of these three forms space is provided for comments by the examiner at the time of his visit. Note should be made of the quality of the facilities and specific deficiencies.

For a more complete and detailed listing of special library facilities, examination should be made of the monographs on library buildings published by the Association of College and Reference Libraries. Another good source is *Planning the University Library Building*, a summary of discussions by librarians, architects, and engineers, edited by Burchard and Associates, and published in 1949.

Name of institution

FORM 6
Libraries
(use one page for each library unit)

1. List below the buildings in which libraries are housed.

BUILDING	NATURE OF LIBRARY SERVICES AND FACILITIES MAINTAINED IN THE BUILDING	ASSIGNABLE SQ. FEET OF FLOOR AREA FOR LIBRARY

2. Reading rooms. List below each library reading room

LOCATION OF READING ROOM AND STUDY HALL	ASSIGNABLE SQUARE FEET OF FLOOR AREA	NUMBER OF SEATS

3. Number of carrells available for research students _____
4. Stack space. List below each space used for library stacks

LOCATION OF STACK SPACE	NUMBER OF VOLUMES SHELVED	LINEAL FEET OF SHELVING	ASSIGNABLE SQUARE FEET OF SPACE	
			Used for stacks	Available for stack expansions

5. Service Area. List below each workroom used for library processes.

BUILDING AND ROOM NUMBER	PRINCIPAL USE OF ROOM	ASSIGNABLE SQ. FT. OF FLOOR AREA	NO. OF STAFF MEMBERS	ASSIGNABLE SQ. FT. PER STAFF MEMBER

Comments by examiner at time of visit to libraries

_____   _____
Examiner   Date

Name of institution

FORM 7

Auditoriums, Theaters, Assembly Halls

(use one page for each hall)

1. Name (or number) of hall _____ Building in which located _____

2. Date of completion _____ Date of last major alteration or improvement

   _____ Type of construction (masonry, wood frame, etc.) _____

   Fire-resistive? _____

3. Principal purposes for which used _____

   _____

4. Number of seats; Main floor _____; Balconies _____; Total _____

5. Stage: Width of proscenium arch _____; Depth of stage _____

   Dimensions of wing: Left _____; Right _____

   Fly gallery? _____ Footlights? _____ Curtain? _____

6. Orchestra pit? _____ Pipe organ? _____

7. Projection equipment? _____ In fire-resistive booth? _____

8. Number of dressing rooms _____ Number of washbowls in dressing rooms

   _____ Lineal feet of mirrors in dressing rooms_____

9. Floor area (sq. ft.) for prop storage and preparation _____

   Floor area (sq. ft.) for costume storage and preparation _____

10. Floor area (sq. ft.) of entrance lobby _____

11. Ticket window? _____ Coat check room? _____ Public rest rooms? _____

12. List or describe other facilities:

Quality of facilities as evaluated by examiner:

_____   _____

Examiner   Date

FORM 8
Gymnasiums, Field House, Armory
(use one page for each separate unit)

1. Usual designation of the facility _____

2. Date of completion _____ Date of last major alteration or improvement _____ Type of construction (masonry, wood frame, etc?) _____

   Fire-resistive _____

3. Principal purposes for which used:

   _____ a. Physical education classes   _____ e. Varsity team practice

   _____ b. Military instruction   _____ f. Spectator sports

   _____ c. Classes in other departments   _____ g. List any others

   _____ d. Intramural games

4. Used by: Men only _____; Women only _____; Both men and women _____.

5. Size of main playing floor or drill area _____

6. Equipment provided for: Basketball _____; tennis _____; indoor softball _____; baseball (hard ball) practice _____; volley ball _____; badminton _____; gymnastics _____; running track _____; (if track, give number of laps to mile _____;) jumping pit _____; list any others.

7. Special rooms: Handball and squash courts? _____; corrective gymnastics? _____; wrestling and boxing? _____; list any others.

8. Swimming pool: Indoor pool? _____ (if yes, give dimensions) _____

            Outdoor pool? _____ (if yes, give dimensions) _____

9. Number of locker rooms for men _____; number for women _____

10. Total number of lockers available: for men _____; for women _____

11. Total number of shower heads in dressing rooms: for men _____; for women _____

12. Number of office rooms for staff _____

13. Number of classrooms _____

14. Seats for spectators: Number at main playing floor _____; number at swimming pool _____; number at special rooms _____.

15. Floor area (sq. ft.) of entrance lobby _____; ticket window? _____;

    coat check room? _____

16. List any other facilities provided in the building.

Comments by examiner on quality of facilities as observed at time of visit.

_____   _____
Examiner   Date

College Facilities for Physical Education, Health Education, and Recreation, published in 1948 by the College Physical Education Association, is a valuable source of information on gymnasiums and field houses. This book discusses in detail standards for the design and construction of physical education plants.

Instructional rooms and offices located in the auditorium, library building, or the gymnasium should have been accounted for either by Form 1 for inventory of instructional rooms or by Form 4 for inventory of offices.

Forms 6 and 7 may be extended so that a record can be made of instructional rooms and offices in the auditorium or library building. Provisions for such notation have been made in Form 8 for the inventory of gymnasium facilities.

No form is being suggested in this *Manual* for museums and exhibition rooms, because of the widely varying characteristics of such facilities depending on the objects on display. For the purpose of most space utilization studies, it would be sufficient to indicate the assignable square feet of floor area used for each museum or exhibition room and the floor area used for servicing and storing the display items. Where a building is devoted exclusively or almost exclusively to museum purposes, a form for additional pertinent information should be designed.

Student Living, Recreational, and Non-Instructional Service Areas

Forms 9, 9-a, 10, 11, and 12 are, respectively, for the inventory of student housing facilities (dormitories), married-student housing facilities, dining halls and cafeterias, social rooms and student union, and student health services. Offices for directors and staff members located within these facilities may be noted in these forms, but should be subjected to detailed inventory in Form 4.

Name of institution

FORM 9
Student Housing Facilities

(use one page for each dormitory building; use FORM 9-a for apartment-type housing units for married couples)

1. Name or designation of housing unit _____; For men or women? _____

2. Date of completion _____; Date of last major alteration or improvement _____; Type of construction (masonry, wood frame, etc.?) _____; Fire-resistive? _____

3. Total number of occupants: (a) Maximum under design standards _____; (b) Maximum under current-practice standards _____; (c) Current-actual _____

4. Number of rooms or suites of rooms that house:

	(a) Under design standards	(b) Under current-practice standards
One student only	_____	_____
Two students	_____	_____
Three students	_____	_____
Four or more students	_____	_____

Average square feet of floor space (all space within a room or suite of rooms, including bathroom, closets, etc.) per occupant in each group of rooms:

One-student rooms	_____	_____
Two-student rooms	_____	_____
Three-student rooms	_____	_____
Rooms for four or more	_____	_____
Average for all rooms	_____	_____

5. Indicate number of each kind of unit room under current-practice standards:

	(a) Without lavatory	(b) With lavatory	(c) With full bath
One-student rooms	_____	_____	_____
Two-student rooms	_____	_____	_____
Three-student rooms	_____	_____	_____
Rooms for four or more	_____	_____	_____

6. The following items refer to common toilet rooms located within the housing unit: Number of toilet rooms _____; Number of toilet stools _____; Number of urinals _____; Number of washbowls _____; Number of shower heads _____; Number of bathtubs _____

7. Floor area of social rooms _____; floor area of student lounges _____

8. Other special rooms provided in the housing unit: Laundry and pressing room? _____; Trunk storage? _____; Library? _____; Suite for matron or proctor? _____; Office of director? _____; Other (list) _____

9. Heat from: Central plant or from plant within building? _____; If heated from plant in building, what kind of fuel is used? _____

10. Location of fire escapes: _____

Quality of facilities as evaluated by examiner at time of visit:

_____ _____

Examiner Date

Name of institution

FORM 9-a
Housing Facilities for Married Students

(use one page for each married student housing area consisting of similar units, i.e., barrack-type duplexes or quonset-type huts, and for each apartment-type building designated for families of married students)

1. Usual designation of housing area or apartment building _____

2. If housing area, date established _____; If apartment building, date com-

   pleted _____; Describe type of construction _____:

   Fire-resistive? _____

3. Total number of family units _____; Number of units now occupied _____

4. Indicate number of kinds of family units in area or building (classification by number of bedrooms should be according to standard for unit as established by college housing office; for example, an apartment listed by office as one-bedroom unit should be so classified, even though student-family may currently be using a living room as a second bedroom):

	WITH KITCHEN AND BATHROOM	WITH KITCHEN ONLY	WITH BATHROOM ONLY
One bedroom and separate living room	_____	_____	_____
One bedroom and no separate living room	_____	_____	_____
Two bedrooms and separate living room	_____	_____	_____
Two bedrooms and no separate living room	_____	_____	_____
Three or more bedrooms	_____	_____	_____

5. Trunk and personal equipment storage: Space provided in each family

   unit _____; Central storage room _____; No storage facilities

   provided _____

6. Community facilities available within housing area or in apartment building:

   Number of washing machines _____ Number of separate clothes dryers _____

   Number of laundry tubs _____ Number of ironing boards _____

7. Heated from: Central plant _____; Heating plant in building _____;

   Stove or furnace in individual family units _____

8. If apartment-type building, location of fire-escapes _____
   Quality of facilities as evaluated by examiner at time of visit:

Examiner	Date

Name of institution

FORM 10

Dining Halls and Cafeterias

(use one page for each dining hall)

1. Usual designation of the dining hall _____

2. Date of completion of building in which dining hall is located _____ ;

   Date of last major alteration or improvement affecting dining hall _____ ;

   Describe type of construction _____ ; Fire-resistive _____

3. Used by: Men only _____ ; women only _____ ; both men and women _____ .

4. Style of service: Table service _____ ; cafeteria _____ ; counter service _____ .

5. Meals served: Breakfast _____ ; Lunch _____ ; Dinner _____ ; Snack bar ____ .

6. Number of tables _____ ; total seating capacity_____

7. Square feet of floor area in dining hall, excluding all service areas _____
8. Service facilities:
   (a) Serving pantry? _____ If yes, give floor area (sq. ft.) _____

   (b) Kitchen: Attached? _____ If yes, give floor area (sq. ft.) _____

   Service from central kitchen located elsewhere? _____

   (c) Food storage: Special storage for meat? ____ Storage for canned goods? ____

   Cold room for fruits and vegetables? ____ Total floor area for food storage ____

   (d) Separate dining room for kitchen help? _____ If yes, give floor area _____
   (e) Other service facilities (list and give sq. ft. floor area)

9. Number of students normally served at: Breakfast _____ ; Lunch _____ ;

   Dinner _____

Quality of facilities as eveluted by examiner at time of visit.

_____   _____
                    Examiner   Date

Name of institution

FORM 11
Social Rooms, Student Union

1. List below the buildings or rooms available for use by entire student body for social purposes (exclude social rooms in dormitories for use of dormitory residents and their guests, and exclude also dining rooms)

BUILDING	PRINCIPAL FACILITIES PROVIDED	SQ. FEET FLOOR AREA (INSIDE GROSS)

2. Check in the list below the kinds of facilities provided by the institution.

_____ a. Lounge

_____ b. Meeting rooms

_____ c. Offices for student organizations

_____ d. Work rooms for student publications

_____ e. Browsing rooms

_____ f. Dance floors

_____ g. Pool and billiards room

_____ h. Bowling alleys

_____ i. Game rooms for ping pong, shuffleboard, etc.

_____ j. Card rooms

_____ k. Little theater

_____ l. Bookstore

_____ m. Barber shop

_____ n. Beauty parlor

_____ o. Other stores or shops

_____ p. Postoffice

_____ q. Hotel rooms for transients

_____ r. Snack bar, soda fountain

_____ s. Others (list)

3. Quality of facilities as evaluated by examiner at time of visit

_____   _____

Examiner   Date

Name of institution

FORM 12

Hospital and Infirmary

(use one page for each separate facility; in items 1 to 7 include only
facilities actually owned and operated by the institution)

1. Usual designation of this facility _____

2. Location: Building _____; floor _____

3. Square feet of floor area (inside gross or assignable) for hospital or infirmary

   purposes _____

4. Number of hospital beds: for men _____; for women _____; total _____

5. Number of beds in isolation ward: for men _____; for women _____; total ____

6. Does infirmary have its own diet kitchen? _____

7. Special rooms provided:

   _____ a. Reception room

   _____ b. Treatment room for non-hospitalized cases

   _____ c. Physical examination room

   _____ d. Dental treatment room

   _____ e. X-Ray room

   _____ f. Operating room for minor surgery

   _____ g. Operating room for major surgery

   _____ h. Nurses' living quarters

   _____ i. Other special rooms: (list)

8. Hospitals in the vicinity, not a part of this institution, available for care of students:

9. Quality of facilities as evaluated by examiner at time of visit

_____   _____

Examiner   Date

Buildings and Grounds Maintenance Space

Form 13 is for the service shops and storerooms used for plant operation and maintenance purposes. As explained earlier, janitorial closets and furnace rooms serving individual buildings should not be included in the category. Office space located in service shops should be processed by Form 4.

Name of institution

FORM 13

Service Shops and Storerooms

List below the facilities for service shops (for plant operation and maintenance) and general storerooms. Use one line for each such facility.

LOCATION	PRINCIPAL USE	SQ. FT. FLOOR AREA (INSIDE GROSS)

Quality of facilities as evaluated by examiner at time of visit.

Examiner   Date

Form 13 might also be used, with appropriate modifications in wording, for the inventory of barns, stables, and shops for the storage and maintenance of agricultural equipment.

Summary Evaluation of All Building Space

Form 14 is for a summary evaluation of the gross floor area of all buildings. The data collected in this form are extremely valuable for planning purposes, and every institution, whether it makes a comprehensive or only a limited study of plant utilization, should attempt to complete Form 14. Because of the importance of these data for capital outlay planning, it is suggested that the ratings be made by a committee consisting of the president, the plant superintendent, and several others familiar with the plant problems of the institution.

Form 14 suggests that the floor area be reported on the basis of gross, or over-all, square feet measurement of the building. For questions relating to replacement and renovations of plant space, the gross floor area is generally a better measure to use than either the inside gross or assignable square feet figure. Form 14, however, can be modified to include all three measures of square feet of floor area for each building.

Each building reported on Form 14 should be designated as either a permanent or a temporary structure and as either fire-resistive or non-fire-resistive. There are no hard and fast rules for determining whether a building is permanent or temporary. A permanent building is usually one that is constructed of some kind of masonry, such as stone, brick, tile, or cement blocks. A temporary structure is usually made of much less durable material, as in the case of barrack-type buildings. Durability of material, however, is not the sole criterion of whether a building is permanent or temporary. Quonset huts, constructed of steel and cement, should last as long as a structure made of masonry, with adequate care. Few institutions, however, would list quonset-type huts among their permanent buildings, particularly if such buildings are being used for classrooms and faculty offices. Suitability of the structure for the purpose used should also be taken into consideration in classifying it as permanent or temporary.

A building identified as "temporary" should ordinarily be rated as either "continue in use for limited time only" or "dis-

FORM 14

Summary Evaluation of the Floor Area of Buildings

(Enter number of square feet in appropriate columns)

Examiner _____   Date _____

NAME OF BUILDING	GROSS SQUARE FEET OF FLOOR AREA	CONSTRUCTION FEATURES			CONTINUE IN SERVICE INDEFINITELY				CONTINUE IN USE FOR LIMITED TIME ONLY	DISCONTINUE USE AT THE EARLIEST OPPORTUNITY
		Permanent or Temporary?	Fire-Resistive? (yes or no)	Masonry, Frame, or Other?	With Only Ordinary Maintenance	Care for Delayed Maintenance (Major)	With Alterations to Adapt to Institutional Program			
							Minor Changes Only	Major Changes		
TOTALS										
Percentage of Total Floor Area in Each Category										

continue use at the earliest opportunity." There are at least five good reasons why a temporary building should be destroyed or removed from the campus. (1) It is nearly always expensive to maintain and to operate. (2) It is usually ill-adapted to institutional needs, particularly as office or instructional space. (3) It usually constitutes a fire hazard for occupants and to other buildings. (4) It is usually unattractive. (5) It takes up land that might be used for permanent buildings.

A building classified as "permanent" would ordinarily fall in the category of "continue in use indefinitely." On occasion an institution might find that it has a building, constructed many decades ago, that is still structurally sound and durable, but is no longer effectively usable for institutional purposes. Rather than spend money on costly alterations, it might be economically advisable to raze it and use the same site for a new building. Such a structure should be rated as "continue in use for limited time only" or "discontinue use at the earliest opportunity."

New or relatively new permanent-type structures would ordinarily fall in the category of "continue in service indefinitely with only ordinary maintenance." A building that has not received proper maintenance for a period of several years will usually be in need of major roof repairs, pointing of masonry, replastering, rewiring, or replacement of plumbing facilities. Any or all of these major repair jobs would throw the building in the category of "continue in service indefinitely with care for delayed maintenance." A building that needs to be remodeled or renovated in order to be continued in service should be rated in the column "with alterations to adapt to institutional programs." This same building, however, should be classified as "continue in use for limited time only" or "discontinue use at the earliest opportunity," if in the judgment of the institution, it would be advisable to raze it, rather than attempt to remodel it.

CHAPTER *5*

Forms for the Analysis
and Interpretation of Data

THE analysis and interpretation of data is the core of all statistical studies. A suitable set of forms greatly facilitates the task of analysis and organizes the data so that they may be more readily interpreted.

The forms for the analysis of space utilization data here presented deal, in the main, only with instructional rooms. Even then, it should be noted, the forms will not be all inclusive nor do they exhaust all possible analyses that can be made of this kind of plant space. They will, however, cover the customary utilization analysis made of instructional rooms.

There are two reasons for limiting the scope of analysis to instructional rooms. First, instructional rooms are the main focus of concern of colleges and universities, with respect to plant problems arising from large enrollment increases. Other kinds of plant facilities also constitute problems, but their solutions are frequently contingent upon or colored by the manner in which the space needs of the instructional programs are met. Secondly, the idea or rationale underlying many of the forms for the analyses and interpretation of data for instructional rooms is applicable to other kinds of plant space. After examining some of the analysis forms, particularly those pertaining to square feet of floor area per occupant or per station, quality ratings, and percentage distribution, an imaginative college official should be able to design similar forms applicable to other kinds of plant space. For such facilities as libraries and gymnasiums, the literature published by the respective professional groups will also suggest many interesting analyses of utilization and space requirement.

The forms for the analysis and interpretation of space utilization data will be given a letter designation, such as "A," "B," or "C," so that they may be distinguished from the data collection forms which were identified by numerical designations.

Utilization Analysis of Instructional Rooms

Form A is for the processing of certain data collected in Form 1 —Inventory of Instructional Rooms and in Form 2—Class Schedule Report, so that they can be readily manipulated for various kinds of analyses pertaining to room use and student-station use. One form is to be used for each instructional room. The upper portion of Form A should be filled out from data reported in Form 1. The cells for number of students occupying the room at each period it is used during the week should be obtained from Form 2, the class schedule reports. The class schedule reports should be grouped according to building and room where the classes were held, and the appropriate data for the day and hour of the class meetings transcribed to Form A.

The periods of the day shown in Form A assume that class meetings begin and end near or on the hour. The form should be modified to conform to institutional schedules whereby class meetings begin and end near or on the half-hour, such as from 9:30 A.M. to 10:30 A.M. It is important to remember that a period is a unit of time approximating an hour. Thus, a class of 20 students that meets on Monday from 9:00 A.M. to 11:00 A.M. should be reported once in the cell for Monday, 9–10 A.M., and once again in the cell Monday, 10–11 A.M. A class of 20 students that meets for an hour and half on Tuesday from 9:00 A.M. to 10:30 A.M. (or 10:20) should be reported once in the cell for Tuesday, 9–10 A.M., and for the remaining half-period this class of 20 students should be reported on a "full-period student equivalent basis," which would mean an entry of 10 students in the cell for Tuesday, 10–11 A.M. If another class of 30 students

Name of institution _____

FORM A

Utilization of Classroom, Teaching Laboratory, or Other Instructional Room, by Days of the Week and Periods of the Day

(use one page for each room)

Building _____ Room number _____ Number of student stations _____

Assignable square feet of floor area _____ Department controlling room _____

Principal use of room _____

Number of Students Occupying Room at Each Period It Is Used during the Week

PERIOD OF THE DAY	DAY OF THE WEEK						TOTAL STUDENT-STATION OCCUPANCY
	Monday	Tuesday	Wednesday	Thursday	Friday	Saturday	
7–8 A.M.							
8–9							
9–10							
10–11							
11–12							
12–1 P.M.							
1–2							
2–3							
3–4							
4–5							
5–6							
6–7							
7–8							
8–9							
9–10							
10–11							
11–12							
TOTAL STUDENT-STATION OCCUPANCY							

ROOM USE:

    a. Total number of periods during week that the room is in use   _____

    b. Average percentage of possible room-period use for week   _____

STUDENT-STATION USE:

    a. Student-hours per station for week   _____

    b. Average percentage of possible student-station-period use for week   _____

    c. Average percentage of student stations occupied in classroom when room is in use _____

59

should meet in the same room on Tuesday from 10:30 A.M. to 12:00 noon, the complete entry for the cell for Tuesday, 10–11 A.M., would be the total enrollments of the first class and the second class adjusted to full-period student equivalents. The complete entry for the cell Tuesday, 10–11 A.M., would thus be 25 students. All classes that meet for only half an hour should also be processed by this same procedure.

The lower part of Form A is for showing some of the more useful measures of utilization for the room, on a weekly basis. In computing the data for "average percentage of possible room-period use for week" and for "average percentage of possible student-station-period use for week" a decision will have to be made whether or not to include classes held either before or after the regularly scheduled college day. These early morning, or late afternoon, or night classes are frequently a part of the on-campus adult education program, and the courses may not be recognized as units of the regular academic programs. They nevertheless constitute a justifiable and scheduled use of campus facilities. If the institution were not to hold such classes on the campus, it would be required to construct or rent off-campus facilities. These classes should therefore be processed as a use of instructional rooms, and reflected in the computation of the percentages of possible utilization. For example, if a room is used for 20 periods during the hours of the regularly scheduled week and is used for 10 additional periods before or after the hours of the regularly scheduled week, the total number of weekly room-periods of use should be shown as 30. In computing the percentage of possible room-period utilization on the basis of a 44-hour weekly schedule, this figure of 30 should be used. It is recommended that the same procedure be followed for computing the average percentage of possible student-station-period use.

Form A, aside from the fact that it is an effective device for processing the data collected in Form 1 and Form 2, presents a quick picture of the utilization for a given room. It is suggested that an institution that allows the various academic units to control the use of rooms prepare duplicate copies of completed Form A and send to each department head the copies of the form for rooms controlled by him, together with suggestions for possible improvements in the utilization of the facilities.

Form B is for a summary of utilization data by kinds of instructional rooms, such as general classrooms and teaching laboratories. The data for this tabulation should be obtained from Form A, except for the figures to be entered in Columns 6 and 10. As a check on the accuracy of the measures of utilization reported in Form A, an institution may choose to transcribe from it only the data for building and room number, number of student stations, total room-periods of use, and total student station occupancy, and re-compute most of the measures. The procedure for computing each of the utilization measures suggested for Form B is as follows:

COLUMN 4. For average at bottom of page for given group of rooms, divide total room periods of use for group (see total at bottom of page for Column 4) by total number of rooms in group (see total at bottom of page for Column 2).

COLUMN 5. Enter number of hours in institution's regular weekly schedule in blank caption space provided for this figure. Divide figure for room reported in Column 4 by the number of hours in weekly schedule, and express quotient as percentage. For average at bottom of page multiply total number of rooms in group (see total for Column 2 bottom of page) by institution's regular weekly schedule, divide the total room periods of use for group (see total for Column 4 at bottom of page) by the resulting product, and express quotient as percentage.

COLUMN 6. Divide figure for room reported in Column 4 by 44 hours and express quotient as percentage. For average for group of rooms multiply total number of rooms in group by 44 hours, divide total room

FORM B

Summary of Utilization Data by Kinds of Instructional Rooms

(Data from Form A; use one page for each kind of instructional room.)

Name of institution

Kind of Instructional Rooms

BUILDING (1)	ROOM NUMBER (2)	NUMBER OF STUDENT-STATIONS (3)	ROOM USE, WEEKLY BASIS			STUDENT-STATION USE, WEEKLY BASIS				
			Total Room-Periods of Use (4)	Percentage of Possible Room-Period Use		Total Student-Station-Periods Occupied (7)	Student Hours per Station (8)	Percentage of Possible Station Use		Percentage of Station Use When Room Actually in Use (11)
				Hrs. Week (5)	44 Hrs. Week (6)			Hrs. Week (9)	44 Hrs. Week (10)	
TOTAL	*									
AVERAGE										

* Report total number of rooms involved.

periods of use for group of rooms by resulting product, and express quotient as percentage.

COLUMN 8. Divide figure for room in Column 7 by figure in Column 3. For average at bottom of page, divide total student-station-periods occupied for group of rooms by total number of student stations in group of rooms.

COLUMN 9. Enter number of hours in institution's regular weekly schedule in blank space provided for this figure. Multiply figure for room in Column 3 by number of hours in institution's schedule, divide figure for room in Column 7 by resulting product, and express quotient as percentage. Another method is to divide the figure for room in Column 8 by the number of hours in institution's weekly schedule, and express quotient as percentage. Compute average at bottom of page by using appropriate total figures for group of rooms.

COLUMN 10. Multiply figure reported for room in Column 3 by 44 hours, divide figure in Column 7 by resulting product, and express quotient as percentage. Another method is to divide figure for room in Column 8 by 44 hours, and express quotient as percentage. Compute average at bottom of page by use of appropriate total figures for group of rooms.

COLUMN 11. Multiply figure for room in Column 4 by figure in Column 3, divide figure in Column 7 by resulting product, and express quotient as percentage. For average at bottom of page, add all the products resulting from multiplication of figure in Column 4 by figure in Column 3 for the individual rooms, divide sum thus obtained into the total student-station-periods occupied for given group of rooms (see total at bottom of page for Column 7), and express quotient as percentage.

Because of the wide variations among institutions in weekly schedules, Form B provides two columns under "percentage of possible room-period use" and "percentage of possible student station use." One column (Columns 5 and 9) is for reporting the percentage of possible utilization, for each of these measures, based on the number of hours in the institution's weekly schedule. It is assumed that in Form A these two measures of utilization would be computed on the basis of the institution's weekly schedule. The second column (Columns 6 and 10) is for showing the percentage of possible utilization as computed on the basis of a week of 44 hours or periods. This weekly schedule of 44 hours is being suggested so that institutions of higher education may over a period of several years develop and exchange utilization data that are comparable. The selection of the exact number of hours is arbitrary, and for many institutions the regular weekly schedule may be longer than 44 hours, while for others it may be shorter.

An institution that has difficulty in identifying its "regular weekly schedule" in terms of a given number of hours, or has any aversion to expressing utilization in terms of percentages of possible use, can omit Columns 5, 6, 9, and 10. Some institutional officials find utilization data much easier to interpret if expressed as percentages of possible use; others prefer to rely chiefly on such measures as "total room periods of use," "average period use per room," and "student hours per station." Until an institution gains considerable familiarity with space utilization data, it is suggested that it attempt to compute all significant measures of use.

After completing Form B for the various kinds of instructional rooms, an institution may wish to compute the summary utilization figures for all rooms combined. This can be done by obtaining a grand total for each of Columns 2, 3, 4, and 7 of all the Form B's, and by subjecting them to the same procedure by which the utilization measures were obtained for the various groups of instructional rooms in Form B.

Form C is the summary of instructional space utilization by the days of the week. It is suggested that this analysis be done for each major category of kinds of instructional rooms and also for all rooms combined. Section "B" of Form C outlines the procedure for deriving the total available room-periods available for each day of the week, as based on the institution's schedule and as based on a 44-period week. Section "D" does the same for student occupancy. The procedure for obtaining each of the utilization measures suggested for Form C is as follows:

COLUMN 1. This figure is the sum of all room-period use for a given day for a given group of instructional rooms. To obtain this figure, the individual Form A's should be grouped into the appropriate categories of instructional rooms, and the numbers of periods of room use for each day tabulated on a work sheet.

COLUMN 2. Divide figure obtained for Column 1 by the number of rooms in group.

COLUMN 3. Divide figure in Column 1 by figure obtained for the day in Section "B-1," and express resulting quotient as percentage.

COLUMN 4. Divide figure in Column 1 by figure obtained for the day in Section "B-2," and express resulting quotient as percentage.

COLUMN 5. This figure is the sum of all student-station-period use for a given day for a given group of instructional rooms. To obtain this figure, the individual Form A's would have to be grouped into appropriate categories of instructional rooms, and number of periods of station use for each day tabulated on a work sheet.

COLUMN 6. Divide figure in Column 5 by total number of student stations in group.

COLUMN 7. Divide figure in Column 5 by total available student-station-periods for day as determined in Section "D-1", and express quotient as percentage.

Name of institution _____

FORM C

Summary of Instructional Room Utilization by Days of the Week

(Data from Form A; use one page for each kind of instructional room)

A. Kind of instructional room _____; total number of rooms _____

B. Total available room-periods each day:

    1. Based on institution's schedule (total rooms times number of periods in institution's daily schedule)

        Mon. _____; Tues. _____; Wed. _____; Thur. _____; Fri. _____; Sat. _____

    2. Based on 44-period week

        Each day, Monday through Friday (total rooms times 8) _____

        Saturday (total rooms times 4) _____

C. Total number of student-stations in this group of rooms _____

D. Total available student-station-periods each day:

    1. Based on the institution's schedule (total student-stations times number of periods in the institution's daily schedule)

        Mon. _____; Tues. _____; Wed. _____; Thur. _____; Fri. _____; Sat. _____

    2. Based on 44-period week

        Each day, Monday through Friday (total student-stations times 8) _____

        Saturday (total student-stations times 4) _____

DAY OF WEEK	ROOM-PERIOD USE				STUDENT-STATION-PERIOD USE			
	Total Room-Periods Used	Average Room-Periods Use for Day	Percentage of Possible Utilization		Total Student-Station-Periods Occupied	Average Student Hours per Station	Percentage of Possible Utilization	
			Based on Institution Schedule	Based on Week of 44 Periods			Based on Institution Schedule	Based on Week of 44 Periods
	(1)	(2)	(3)	(4)	(5)	(6)	(7)	(8)
Monday								
Tuesday								
Wednesday								
Thursday								
Friday								
Saturday								

Column 8. Divide figure in Column 5 by total available student-station-periods for day as determined in Section "D-2", and express quotient as percentage.

Form C serves two purposes. One is to determine the rates of scheduled utilization of instructional space for each day of the week. The second, and by far the more significant, is to detect variations in the rates of scheduled utilization among the days of the week. Most institutions make better use of their instructional rooms on Mondays, Wednesdays, and Fridays, than on Tuesdays and Thursdays. There are many explanations for this pattern, but none of them constitutes a valid excuse for failure to use the facilities as efficiently on Tuesdays and Thursdays, as on Mondays, Wednesdays, and Fridays. Certain of the rates of utilization for Saturdays tend to be low, chiefly because most institutions that schedule classes on this day do so only for the morning hours.

It is to be noted that Form C does not suggest an analysis of the percentage of student-station-period use in rooms when the rooms are actually used. This measure serves primarily as an index of the "fit" of the size of a room to the size of classes. It is very useful for the planning of new instructional rooms, but as a guide for improving the utilization of existing facilities, it is of less significance than the measure of "student hours per station" or "the percentage of possible student-station utilization." If an institution suspects that classes tend to be smaller on certain days of the week (or at certain hours of the day) than on other days, a more effective method of testing this hypothesis would be to make a comparison of the average sizes of classes by the days of the week (or by the hours of the day), rather than by computing utilization of student stations in occupied rooms, by the days of the week (or by the hours of day).

Form D is for a summary of instructional space utilization by the hours of the day. The procedures for deriving the total available room-periods and the total available student-station-period

Name of institution _____

FORM D

Summary of Instructional Space Utilization by Hours of the Day

(Data from Form A; use page for each kind of instructional rooms)

A. Kind of instructional rooms _____ ; total number of rooms _____

B. Total available room-periods weekly at each hour:

1. Based on institution's schedule (For each hour, enter in first column the number of rooms in category times number of days in the week classes may meet at that hour.)

2. Based on 44-period week (Enter in 2nd column.)

   a. Morning hours (number of rooms in category times 6) _____

   b. Afternoon hours (number of rooms in category times 5) _____

C. Total number of student-stations in this group of rooms _____

D. Total available student-station-periods weekly at each hour:

1. Based on institution's schedule (For each hour, enter in 3rd column number of student stations in category times number of days in the week classes may meet at that hour.)

2. Based on 44-period week (Enter in 4th column.)

   a. Morning hours (number of student stations times 6) _____

   b. Afternoon hours (number of student stations times 5) _____

HOUR OF DAY	TOTAL AVAILABLE ROOM-PERIODS		TOTAL AVAILABLE STATION-PERIODS		TOTAL ROOM PERIODS USED	TOTAL STUDENT-STATION-PERIODS OCCUPIED WEEKLY	PERCENTAGE OF POSSIBLE UTILIZATION			
							Room-Period Basis		Student-Station-Period Basis	
	Based on Instit. Schedule (1)	Based on Week of 44 Periods (2)	Based on Instit. Schedule (3)	Based on Week of 44 Periods (4)	(5)	(6)	Based on Instit. Schedule (7)	Based on Week of 44 Periods (8)	Based on Instit. Schedule (9)	Based on Week of 44 Periods (10)
7–8 A.M.		X		X				X		X

68

8–9										
9–10										
10–11										
11–12										
12–1 P.M.		X		X				X		X
1–2										
2–3										
3–4										
4–5										
5–6		X		X				X		X
6–7		X		X				X		X
7–8		X		X				X		X
8–9		X		X				X		X
9–10		X		X				X		X
10–11		X		X				X		X
11–12		X		X				X		X

occupancy, so that the rates of possible utilization can be computed, are outlined in the upper part of the form. Classes that are held either before or after the regular institutional day may be included in this analysis. If they are to be included, the total available room-periods and the total available student-station-periods for the hour or hours when they are held should be computed in the same manner as for other hours.

Another method of examining the use of instructional facilities for each hour of the day is to compute the percentage distribution of total room-period-occupancy and the total student-station-period occupancy by the hours of the day. Form D-a suggests the manner in which this analysis might be made.

The results of most utilization studies for collegiate institutions indicate that the morning hours have far better usage of instructional space than the hours after 12:00 noon. Student and faculty preference for morning classes has been suggested as a major contributing factor to this pattern.

A careful examination of the results of Forms C and D will frequently show that by imaginative scheduling of classes, an institution can accommodate large increases in enrollments with its present instructional facilities and even within its current weekly schedule. Peter Masiko in the May, 1956, issue of *College and University Business*, suggests a pattern of class scheduling that permits an almost complete utilization of room-periods. A longer weekly schedule is, of course, another method for accommodating enrollment increases.

Form E is for a summary of utilization of instructional space in rooms of various sizes. Size in this instance pertains to the number of student stations located in a room. The measures of utilization suggest which rooms, grouped according to size, are used more efficiently than others.

Form F gives another perspective of the relationship of class size to room size. Simply put, this is an analysis of "fit" or compatibility. The entries in cells above the heavy black line show the number of class-period meetings in which the classes were

Name of institution

FORM D-a (data from Form A)

Percentage Distribution of Total Room Periods Scheduled for Each Hour of the Day and of Total Student-Station-Period Occupancy for Each Hour of the Day

Kind of Instructional Rooms Involved _____

HOURS OF THE DAY	ROOM-PERIOD USE			STUDENT-STATION-PERIOD OCCUPANCY		
	Total Number at Each Hour	Percentage of Total		Total Number at Each Hour	Percentage of Total	
		At Each Hour	Cumulative		At Each Hour	Cumulative
7–8 A.M.						
8–9						
9–10						
10–11						
11–12						
12–1 P.M.						
1–2						
2–3						
3–4						
4–5						
5–6						
6–7						
7–8						
8–9						
9–10						
10–11						
11–12						
TOTAL		100.0			100.0	

compatible with or larger than the number of student stations found in the room at the time the inventory of stations was made. Entries below the heavy black line show the extent to which classes were smaller than the seating capacity of the rooms in which they were held.

The data in Forms E and F, properly interpreted, can be used in determining the number of classrooms of each size to include

Name of institution ___

FORM E (data from Form A)

Summary of Utilization of Instructional Space in Rooms of Each Size

(use one page for each kind of instructional rooms)

Kind of Instructional Rooms ___

NUMBER OF STUDENT STATIONS IN ROOM	NUMBER OF ROOMS OF EACH SIZE	TOTAL AVAILABLE ROOM PERIODS		TOTAL STUDENT STATIONS IN EACH GROUP OF ROOMS	TOTAL AVAILABLE STUDENT-STATION PERIODS		ROOM-PERIOD USE				STUDENT-STATION-PERIOD USE				
		Based on Instit. Schedule	Based on Week of 44 Periods		Based on Instit. Schedule	Based on Week of 44 Periods	Total Room-Periods Used	Average Room-Periods Use for Week	Percentage of Possible Utilization: Based on Instit. Schedule	Based on Week of 44 Periods	Total Student-Station-Periods Occupied	Average Student Hours per Week per Station	Percentage of Possible Utilization: Based on Instit. Schedule	Based on Week of 44 Periods	Per Cent of Station Use When Room in Use
	(1)	(2)	(3)	(4)	(5)	(6)	(7)	(8)	(9)	(10)	(11)	(12)	(13)	(14)	(15)
1–10															
11–20															
21–30															
31–40															

	41–50	51–60	61–80	81–100	101–150	151–200	201–250	251 and Over

Name of institution _____

FORM F (data from Form A)

Distribution of the Number of Class-Period Meetings per Week by Size of Class in Relationship to Capacity of the Room in Which Classes Are Held

Kind of Instructional Rooms _____

ROOM CAPACITY	NUMBER OF CLASS-PERIOD MEETINGS PER WEEK FOR CLASSES OF EACH GROUP												TOTAL	PERCENTAGE	CUMULATIVE PERCENTAGE
	1 to 10	11 to 20	21 to 30	31 to 40	41 to 50	51 to 60	61 to 80	81 to 100	101 to 150	151 to 200	201 to 250	251 and Over			
1 to 10															
11 to 20															
21 to 30															
31 to 40															
41 to 50															
51 to 60															
61 to 80															
81 to 100															
101 to 150															
151 to 200															
201 to 250															
251 and Over															
TOTAL															
PERCENTAGE															
CUMULATIVE PERCENTAGE															

in new instructional buildings. It should be noted, however, that the need to economize in the use of faculty manpower may in the future require institutions to increase the average size of classes in most subject-fields considerably beyond the present levels. Plans for new instructional facilities should take into account not only the data in Forms E and F, but also probable changes in instructional methods that would affect the sizes of classrooms.

Forms G and H are for the purpose of measuring the relative efficiency in utilization between instructional rooms assigned to departments and for unassigned rooms, and among the departments that have rooms permanently assigned to them. Form G provides for this analysis on a room-period basis and Form H, on a student-station basis. Only departments that have one or more instructional rooms permanently assigned to them should be listed. Permanent assignment, in this instance, means the same as control.

The data of this analysis frequently indicate that the policy of assigning rooms permanently to departments results in less effective use of such facilities than when rooms are controlled by a central institutional office and are assigned as needed to each department for specific classes. When an instructional room is permanently assigned to a department, it becomes identified with that department so strongly that other departments hesitate to ask for its use or the controlling department comes to interpret requests from other departments for its use as encroachments on its domain.

The designation of a building is another factor that seems to affect the rates of utilization of instructional rooms. In a plant utilization study of seven New Mexico state-supported institutions, it was found that buildings that were named after the subject-fields taught in them, such as "chemistry building," "home economics building," or "education building," generally had a lower rate of use than buildings that were named after persons, such as past presidents or donors. There is no reason why a general lecture room located in the "chemistry building" or the

Name of institution

FORM G (data from Form A)
Analysis of Room-Period Utilization by Instructional Departments to Which Rooms Are Permanently Assigned

DEPARTMENTS OR OFFICE TO WHICH ROOMS ARE PERMANENTLY ASSIGNED (LIST UNASSIGNED ROOMS ON LINE "a", AND DEPARTMENTS TO WHICH ROOMS ARE PERMANENTLY ASSIGNED ON LINE "b" AND FOLLOWING)	GENERAL CLASSROOMS		TEACHING LABORATORIES		OTHERS	
	Number of Rooms	Per Cent Room-period Use on 44-hour Week Basis*	Number of Rooms	Per Cent Room-period Use on 44-hour Week Basis*	Number of Rooms	Per Cent Room-period Use on 44-hour Week Basis*
a. Unassigned rooms						
b. Department						
c. "						
d. "						
e. "						
f. "						
g. "						
h. "						
i. "						
j. "						
k. "						
l. "						
m. "						
n. "						
o. "						
p. "						
q. "						
r. "						
s. "						
t. "						
TOTAL FOR INSTITUTION						

* Instead of this measure, may use "average number of periods per week per room," or may compute both measures.

"home economics building" cannot be used for classes in English, history, mathematics, or education. But the mere fact that a building is named after a subject-field tends to restrict the use of its facilities to one department. It is usually only through a policy

Name of institution

FORM H (data from Form A)

Analysis of Student-station Utilization by Instructional Departments to which Rooms Are Permanently Assigned

DEPARTMENT OR OFFICE TO WHICH ROOMS ARE PERMANENTLY ASSIGNED (LIST UNASSIGNED ROOMS ON LINE "a", AND DEPARTMENTS TO WHICH ROOMS ARE PERMANENTLY ASSIGNED ON LINE "b" AND FOLLOWING)	GENERAL CLASSROOMS			TEACHING LABORATORIES			OTHERS		
	Number of Student-stations	Per Cent Station-period Use on 44-hr. Week*	Per Cent Station-period Use When Room in Use	Number of Student-stations	Per Cent Station-period Use on 44-hr. Week*	Per Cent Station-period Use When Room in Use	Number of Student-stations	Per Cent Station-period Use on 44-hr. Week*	Per Cent Station-period Use When Room in Use
a. Unassigned rooms									
b. Department									
c. "									
d. "									
e. "									
f. "									
g. "									
h. "									
i. "									
j. "									
k. "									
l. "									
m. "									
n. "									
o. "									
p. "									
q. "									
r. "									
s. "									
TOTAL FOR INSTITUTION									

* Instead of this measure, may use "average number of student hours per week per station," or may compute both measures.

of central institution-wide control of all instructional facilities that full use can be made of classrooms located in such a building. The comparison of the utilization of instructional rooms by buildings in which they are located can be done on Form B, by organizing the rooms of given kind into sub-groups by buildings and computing the totals and averages for each sub-group. With appropriate modifications, Forms G and H can also be used to make this comparative analysis by buildings.

Form J is for a summary of square feet of assignable floor space per 100 hours of student occupancy. Institutions tend to

---

Name of institution

FORM J (data from Form A)
Summary of Square Feet of Assignable Floor Space per 100 Hours of Student Occupancy

KINDS OF INSTRUCTIONAL ROOMS	NUMBER OF ROOMS	ASSIGNABLE SQUARE FEET OF FLOOR SPACE	HOURS OF STUDENT OCCUPANCY	SQUARE FEET OF FLOOR SPACE PER 100 HOURS OF STUDENT OCCUPANCY
General classrooms				
Teaching laboratories				
a. *				
b.				
c.				
d.				
e.				
f.				
Other rooms (specify)				
a. *				
b.				
c.				
All rooms combined				

* Fill in with appropriate sub-category.

---

vary in the average amounts of floor space allotted per student station for the various kinds of instructional rooms, some being more generous than others. It is thus possible that an institution with a higher rate of existing student station utilization than another may have less efficient use of instructional space because of poor planning in the placement of equipment and stations or in the design of the room. The analysis of square feet of assignable floor space per a given number of hours of student occupany is, however, a rather recent innovation, and until its application becomes more widespread, an institution may have difficulty in obtaining data resulting from such analyses for other institutions for the purpose of making comparisons.

Form K is for a summary of assignable square feet of floor area per student station in rooms for each major purpose—general classrooms, teaching laboratories, and others. For "teaching laboratories" and "others," space for sub-categories of instructional rooms is provided. Data on square feet of floor area per student station for each room are obtainable from Form 1—Inventory of Instructional Rooms.

The kinds of analyses of instructional rooms suggested by Forms A to K are by no means exhaustive. There are others that can be made from the data collected in Form 1—Inventory of Instructional Rooms and from Form 2—Class Schedule Report, and that should be made, if pertinent to the instructional space problems of the institution.

Quality Ratings of Instructional Rooms

Poor facilities can rarely be used as extensively and as effectively as good facilities. The deterrents are both physical and psychological. A classroom that is lacking in proper equipment, such as chalkboards, adequate artificial lighting, and good ventilation, cannot be used for certain kinds of classes or at certain times of the day or year. And at the insistence of faculty members or students, those responsible for scheduling classes tend to avoid the use of rooms that are unpleasant in appearance and lacking in comfort. The factor of quality of instructional rooms should therefore always be borne in mind in interpreting low rates of utilization, or in setting standards for minimum utilization.

Name of institution

FORM K (data from Form 1)

Summary of Assignable Square Feet of Floor Area per Student-Station in Rooms for Each Major Purpose

NUMBER OF ASSIGNABLE SQUARE FEET PER STUDENT-STATION	STATIONS IN GENERAL CLASSROOMS		STATIONS IN TEACHING LABORATORIES										STATIONS IN OTHER ROOMS			
			(a)*		(b)*		(c)*		(d)*		(e)*		(a)†		(b)†	
	Number	Per Cent	Number	Per Cent	Number	Per Cent	Number	Per Cent	Number	Per Cent	Number	Per Cent	Number	Per Cent	Number	Per Cent
9 or less																
10– 14.9																
15– 19.9																
20– 24.9																
25– 29.9																
30– 39.9																
40– 49.9																

50– 59.9												
60– 79.9												
80– 99.9												
100–124.9												
125–149.9												
150–174.9												
175–199.9												
200 or more												
TOTAL	100.0	100.0	100.0	100.0	100.0	100.0	100.0	100.0	100.0	100.0	100.0	100.0
AVERAGE (MEAN)												

* Fill in with appropriate designation of sub-category, such as for engineering, home economics, science, arts & crafts, etc.

† Fill in with appropriate designation of sub-category, such as music practice rooms.

Forms L-a, L-b, L-c, and L-d are for the summary of quality ratings of instructional rooms. The basic data for completing these forms are obtainable from Form 3. The instructional rooms are divided into three major groups—general classrooms, teach-

---

Name of institution

FORM L-a (data from Form 3)
Summary of Quality Rating of Rooms for Instructional Purposes

ITEMS RATED	GEN-ERAL CLASS-ROOMS	TEACHING LABORATORIES					OTHERS		ALL INSTR. SPACE
		(a)*	(b)*	(c)*	(d)*	(e)*	(a)*	(b)*	
Number of rooms: Relation of number of student stations to floor area: a. Overcrowded room b. Space tightly used but adequate c. Comfortable amount of space d. More space than necessary									
TOTAL									
Percentage of rooms: Relation of number of student stations to floor area: a. Overcrowded room b. Space tightly used but adequate c. Comfortable amount of space d. More space than necessary									
TOTAL	100.0%	100.0	100.0	100.0	100.0	100.0	100.0	100.0	100.0%

NOTE: This analysis is on a room basis. By noting the number of student stations in each room, this schedule can be used with minor modifications to show the percentage of student stations affected by the ratings.

* Fill in with appropriate designation of sub-category, such as engineering labs, science labs, home economics labs, etc.

ing laboratories, and others. For teaching laboratories and others, space is provided for sub-categories.

Form L-a pertains to the relationship of number of student stations to the floor area. The data in this table should be interpreted

---

Name of institution

FORM L-b (data from Form 3)
Summary of Quality Rating of Rooms for Instructional Purposes

ITEMS RATED	GENERAL CLASS-ROOMS	TEACHING LABORATORIES					OTHERS		ALL INSTR. SPACE
		(a)*	(b)*	(c)*	(d)*	(e)*	(a)*	(b)*	
Numbers of rooms:									
Quality of accommodations for principal purpose:									
a. Excellent									
b. Satisfactory									
c. Poor									
d. Very deficient									
TOTAL									
Percentage of rooms:									
Quality of accommodations for principal purpose:									
a. Excellent									
b. Satisfactory									
c. Poor									
d. Very deficient									
TOTAL	100.0%	100.0	100.0	100.0	100.0	100.0	100.0	100.0	100.0%

NOTE: This analysis is on a room basis. By noting the number of student stations in each room, this schedule can be used with minor modifications to show the percentage of student stations affected by the ratings.

* Fill in with appropriate designation of sub-category.

in conjunction with the rates for student-station-period utilization. A high proportion of instructional rooms in the categories of "overcrowded room" and "space tightly used but adequate," coupled with a high rate of student-station-period use, would constitute a strong argument for additional space. But an institution with a high proportion of rooms in the categories "comfortable amount of space" and "more space than necessary," would not have much support for additional space, except when its rate of utilization is unusually high or when it has a large amount of

---

Name of institution

FORM L-c (data from Form 3)

Summary of Quality Rating of Rooms for Instructional Purposes

ITEMS RATED	GENERAL CLASS-ROOMS	TEACHING LABORATORIES					OTHERS		ALL INSTR. SPACE
		(a)*	(b)*	(c)*	(d)*	(e)*	(a)*	(b)*	
Number of rooms: General impression of the room: a. Pleasant and attractive b. Satisfactory c. Dreary, unattractive									
TOTAL									
Percentage of rooms: General impression of the room: a. Pleasant and attractive b. Satisfactory c. Dreary, unattractive									
TOTAL	100.0%	100.0	100.0	100.0	100.0	100.0	100.0	100.0	100.0%

NOTE: This analysis is on a room basis. By noting the number of student stations in each room, this schedule can be used with minor modifications to show the percentage of student stations affected by the ratings.

* Fill in with appropriate designation of sub-category.

---

poor quality space, such as temporary buildings and old, ill-adapted structures. Rooms rated in the category of "more space than necessary," if located in structurally sound building units, should be further investigated for the possibility of increasing the number of student stations, if there is need to serve a larger number of students.

Form L-b deals with the quality of accommodations for principal purpose. A high proportion of rooms rated as "poor" or "very deficient" in this respect would be evidence in support of an increased budget for the purchase of new instructional equipment.

Name of institution

FORM L-d (data from Form 3)
Summary of Quality Rating of Rooms for Instructional Purposes

ITEMS RATED	GENERAL CLASS-ROOMS	TEACHING LABORATORIES					OTHERS		ALL INSTR. SPACE
		(a)*	(b)*	(c)*	(d)*	(e)*	(a)*	(b)*	
Number of rooms: Number of specific deficiencies noted in room:									
a. None									
b. 1 or 2 deficiencies									
c. 3 or 4 deficiencies									
d. 5 or more									
TOTAL									
Percentage of rooms: Number of specific deficiencies noted in room:									
a. None									
b. 1 or 2 deficiencies									
c. 3 or 4 deficiencies									
d. 5 or more									
TOTAL	100.0%	100.0	100.0	100.0	100.0	100.0	100.0	100.0	100.0%

NOTE: This analysis is on a room basis. By noting the number of student stations in each room this schedule can be used with minor modifications to show the percentage of student stations affected by the ratings.

* Fill in with appropriate designation of sub-category.

Form L-c summarizes the quality ratings for the general impression of the room. A high proportion of rooms rated as "dreary, unattractive" would ordinarily indicate that the institution has delayed maintenance, or possibly extensive remodeling and renovation of classroom units is needed. If the low-rated rooms are located in temporary units or dilapidated buildings, the better solution might be to raze the structures and replace them with new units.

Form L-d pertains to the summary of number of specific deficiencies noted. If an institution finds that a high percentage of its instructional rooms have three or more specific deficiencies, it should make an analysis of the frequency of occurrence of each specific deficiency. It may, for example, find that a large number of rooms have inadequate lighting, or poor seating arrangements, or are not properly shaped for the kinds of instructional activities for which they are being used. Each of these specific deficiencies calls for different lines of action. Inadequate lighting can be corrected by replacement of light fixtures. Poor seating arrangements can usually be corrected by shifting chairs, except in the case of fixed stations. Rooms that are poorly shaped constitute a form of deficiency that generally can be corrected only by extensive and costly remodeling.

These forms by no means exhaust the kinds of qualitative analysis that can be made of instructional rooms. For example, the rooms and the floor areas can be classified into those located in permanent or temporary buildings, and classified into those housed in permanent buildings that are of recent construction, or in need of remodeling and renovation, or old and unserviceable.

Analyses of Facilities Other than Instructional Rooms

Forms M to R, inclusive, are illustrative of various analyses that can be made of office space, gymnasium facilities, and dormitories. The techniques suggested by the forms are applicable to many other kinds of plant space, such as library reading rooms, library carrells, dining halls and cafeterias, rest rooms, auditoriums, and student health clinics.

Forms M, N, O, and P are for the analyses of data pertaining to office space. In each of these forms, the offices are grouped into three categories—for administrative units, for faculty and staffs of the academic departments, and for other institutional units.

Subcategories may be shown under "other units," such as library staff, organized research units, etc., but this would complicate the analysis. Most institutions will find that the majority of its total office space would be accounted for by the administrative units and the faculty and staffs of the academic departments. For the purposes of Forms M, N, O, and P, it is suggested that the office and the office-station be classified in the category with which the occupant is principally identified. Principal identification of oc-

---

Name of institution

FORM M (data from Form 4)
Summary of Rooms and Floor Space Used for Offices

	ADMINISTRA-TIVE UNITS	FACULTY AND STAFFS OF ACADEMIC DEPTS.	OTHER UNITS (DESCRIBE, IF ANY)	TOTAL FOR INSTITUTION
Number of rooms used				
Number of office-stations				
Total square feet of floor space used				
Average square feet of floor space per station				
Ratio of square feet of office space to total square feet of instructional space				

---

cupant can be determined by either one or both of two kinds of data, (1) the staff member's own judgment of his principal function, or what others believe to be his chief function, and (2) the distribution of his salary between or among the budgets for two or more functions. If a staff member has a different office for each function, there is no need to determine his principal identification.

The analysis features of Form M applicable to a number of other kinds of plant space are the average square feet of floor space per station and the ratio of square feet of office space to total square feet of instructional space. For example, the average square feet of floor space per station may be computed for research laboratories, for dormitories, for cafeteria and dining halls, for library reading rooms, for library carrells, for spectator seating

---

Name of institution

FORM N (data from Form 4)
Square Feet of Floor Space Assigned to Each Office-Station

RANGE IN SQUARE FEET OF FLOOR SPACE	ADMINISTRATIVE UNITS	FACULTY AND STAFF OF ACADEMIC DEPARTMENTS	OTHER UNITS	SUMMARY FOR INSTITUTION
Number of office-stations provided with following square feet of floor space:				
less than 50				
50 to 74				
75 to 99				
100 to 124				
125 to 149				
150 to 199				
200 to 249				
250 or more				
TOTAL				
Percentage of office stations provided with following square feet of floor space:				
less than 50				
50 to 74				
75 to 99				
100 to 124				
125 to 149				
150 to 199				
200 to 249				
250 or more				
TOTAL	100.0%	100.0%	100.0%	100.0%

---

areas, for auditoriums and theatres, and for rest rooms and lounges.

Form N is for showing the numbers and percentages of office

stations provided with varying square feet of floor area. This is a simple device for indicating range and distribution, and in college plant surveys, it is particularly applicable to offices, classrooms, and dormitory rooms.

Name of institution

FORM O (data from Form 4)
Distribution of Office Rooms by Number of Stations per Room

STATIONS PER ROOM	ADMINISTRATIVE UNITS	FACULTY AND STAFF OF ACADEMIC DEPARTMENTS	OTHER UNITS	SUMMARY FOR INSTITUTION
Number of office rooms with following number of stations per room: 1 office-station 2 office-stations 3 office-stations 4 office-stations 5 office-stations 6 or more				
TOTAL NUMBER OF ROOMS				
Percentage of office rooms with following number of stations per room: 1 office-station 2 office-stations 3 office-stations 4 office-stations 5 office-stations 6 or more				
TOTAL	100.0%	100.0%	100.0%	100.0%

Form O provides for an analysis of office rooms by number of person-stations located in each room. This same form can be adapted for a similar analysis of data for student dormitory facilities.

Form P is for a summary of the quality ratings of rooms used

Name of institution _____

FORM P (data from Form 4)
Summary of Quality Ratings of Rooms Used for Offices

ITEMS RATED	NUMBER OF OFFICE-STATIONS AFFECTED				PERCENTAGE OF OFFICE-STATIONS AFFECTED			
	Administrative Units	Faculty and Staff of Academic Departments	Other Units	Total for Institution	Administrative Units	Faculty and Staff of Academic Departments	Other Units	Total for Institution
1. Adequacy of space for number assigned								
a. Excellent								
b. Average								
c. Poor								
TOTAL					100.0%	100.0%	100.0%	100.0%
2. Provisions for privacy								
a. Excellent								
b. Average								
c. Poor								
TOTAL					100.0%	100.0%	100.0%	100.0%

3. General attractiveness of room							
a. Excellent							
b. Average							
c. Poor							
Total		100.0%	100.0%	100.0%	100.0%		
4. Quality of accommodations							
a. Excellent							
b. Average							
c. Poor							
Total		100.0%	100.0%	100.0%	100.0%		
5. Adequacy of lighting,							
a. Excellent							
b. Average							
c. Poor							
Total		100.0%	100.0%	100.0%	100.0%		

for offices. An institution should not feel held to these particular items for determining the quality of an office, and experimentation may indicate that some others would be more reliable indices of quality.

Form Q is suggestive of the kinds of analyses that can be made of special equipment, such as lockers and showerheads. This technique of relating the number of units of a particular item of equipment or number of person-stations to the total number of potential users has wide application in a college plant survey.

Name of institution

FORM Q (data from Form 8)
Analysis of Selected Physical Education Equipment in Relation to Student Enrollment

SPECIAL PHYSICAL EDUCATION EQUIPMENT	TOTAL NUMBER AVAILABLE FOR STUDENT USE	NUMBER OF STUDENTS (HEAD COUNT) PER EACH FACILITY	NUMBER OF STUDENTS REQUIRED TO TAKE PHYSICAL EDUCATION PER EACH FACILITY
Men: Lockers Shower heads			
Women: Lockers Shower heads			

Form R is for a summary of selected data pertaining to student housing facilities. The technique of relating the number of person-stations to the quality of facilities was previously demonstrated for offices in Form P. If a quality rating for individual dormitory rooms is desired, the data collection form for offices (Form 4) can, with minor modification, be adapted to dormitories, and the data analyzed along the lines suggested in Form P. Part 2 of Form R illustrates the technique of analyzing rooms on the basis of unit capacity. Part 3 of Form R represents an application of the analysis technique of relating person-units to square feet of floor space, to dormitory facilities.

Name of institution

FORM R (data from Form 9)
Summary of Student Housing Facilities (excluding facilities for families of married students)

HOUSING ITEM	MEN		WOMEN		TOTAL	
	Number	Per Cent	Number	Per Cent	Number	Per Cent
1. Number and percentage of students housed in institutional facilities who live in buildings of each kind of construction a. Fire-resistive						
b. Masonry, non-fire resistive						
c. Frame (permanent)						
d. Frame (temporary)						
2. Number and percentage of dormitory rooms with following student-units per room: a. 1 student to the room						
b. 2 students to the room						
c. 3 students to the room						
d. 4 or more students to the room						
3. Number and percentage of dormitory student-units with following assignable square feet of floor area: a. Less than 75 square feet per unit						
b. 75–99 square feet per unit						
c. 100–124 square feet per unit						
d. 125–150 square feet per unit						
e. Over 150 square feet per unit						

CHAPTER 6

Normative Data
for Space Utilization

D ATA obtained from a space utilization study generally have greater meaning to an institution if comparisons can be made with the experiences of other institutions in the use of their plant facilities. Such comparisons require normative data based on strictly comparable statistics from studies of space utilization in a substantial number of colleges and universities.

Requirements of Satisfactory Normative Data

There are four minimum requirements for the establishment of satisfactory normative data for space utilization. The first requisite is a system for classifying plant space into various categories, for collecting data, and for measuring utilization on a uniform basis. This *Manual* is intended to establish such a system.

A second requisite is the collection of space utilization data for a large enough group of institutions so that the addition of more data would have no significant effect on measures of central tendencies. In short, satisfactory normative data should be characterized by stability.

A third requisite is the collection and organization of data for groups of comparable institutions. The institutional characteristics to be used as bases for organizing the normative data should be limited to those that are either known or suspected of being factors associated with the degree of use of plant facilities. Considerable research may be necessary before all such factors can be identified and the extent of association properly established.

A fourth requisite for satisfactory normative data for space utilization is recency. Past experiences of institutions suggest that normative data for space utilization, once established, might not become obsolete as quickly as some other kinds of institutional data. Ordinarily it might suffice to re-examine and renew normative data for space utilization once every ten years, or at even longer intervals. But the accelerated enrollment increases and the pressure for greater economy and efficiency in institutional operation, that currently confront higher education, can be expected to bring about rapid and possibly unforeseen changes in space utilization practices. Thus it is highly probable that during the decades of the 1960's and 1970's normative data for college space utilization should be collected as frequently as every five or six years, to be of greatest value as guides for administrative action.

Instructional Space Utilization Data for 101 Institutions

The establishment of norms for space utilization that fully meet all four requirements is not possible at this time. As previously reported, a survey, made in connection with the preparation of this *Manual*, of available college space utilization studies showed that institutions have varied considerably in their definitions of space categories and in the methods of collecting data used to derive the measures of utilization. As a modest beginning, however, toward the preparation of satisfactory norms, utilization data for instructional rooms and student stations for 101 institutions are presented in this *Manual*. The measures of instructional space utilization for each of these institutions appear to have been collected and computed by procedures reasonably comparable to those recommended in this *Manual*.

Included in the 101 institutions are 30 publicly controlled degree-granting colleges and universities, 35 privately controlled degree-granting institutions, 35 publicly controlled junior colleges, and 1 privately controlled junior college. The junior colleges comprising this group all have sole use of their physical plants. Seventy-six of the 101 institutions are from two Pacific Coast states, 7 from five Midwestern states, 7 from a Southwestern state, and 11 from a Southern state. The reports for these 101 institutions leave much to be desired in the way of adequate regional representation, but an examination of the data suggests no consistent pattern of variation in utilization rates that might be interpreted as associated with geographical location of institutions, especially after other factors have been taken into account.

The utilization data for the 101 institutions are all for the fall term or semester. For 3 institutions, the data are for the fall of 1951; for 93, for the fall of 1953; for 1, for the fall of 1954, and for the remaining 4, for the fall of 1955. In view of the fact that most institutions over the country were just beginning to experience enrollment increases in the fall of 1953, following the temporary enrollment decline brought about by the departure of World War II veterans from the campuses, it is quite likely the current space utilization rates for these same institutions might be somewhat higher than those reported in this *Manual*. But most institutions have probably constructed some additional academic space since the utilization study was made, so this would counterbalance the effect of increased enrollment on the utilization figures.

In the tabulations to follow, the utilization data are grouped into those for general classrooms, teaching laboratories, and for all instructional rooms combined, this last being an aggregate for the first two groups. For each of these groupings of instructional space, three measures of utilization are shown—(1) room-period use, expressed as the average number of periods per week per room; (2) student-station-period use, expressed as the average number of student hours per week per station; and (3) the percentage of student-stations used when the rooms are actually occupied. Although the data obtained are from space utilization reports for 101 institutions, no one tabulation in this chapter represents this entire group. The maximum number of institutions represented in a single tabulation is 90. The reason for this is that the three aforementioned utilization measures were not obtainable for each of the three groupings of instructional space for all 101 institutions. A number of institutions, for example, computed only one or two measures of utilization. Also, some institutions did not make a distinction between general classrooms and teaching laboratories but dealt with the single category of all instruc-

TABLE 3
Percentile Ranking of Room-Period Utilization Scores,
Based on 90 Institutions

PER-CENTILE RANK	GENERAL CLASSROOMS		TEACHING LABORATORIES*		ALL INSTRUCTIONAL ROOMS	
	Average Number of Periods per Week per Room	Percentage of Possible Utilization on 44-Hour Weekly Basis	Average Number of Periods per Week per Room	Percentage of Possible Utilization on 44-Hour Weekly Basis	Average Number of Periods per Week per Room	Percentage of Possible Utilization on 44-Hour Weekly Basis
99	42.0	95.5	33.0	75.0	36.0	81.8
90	28.5	64.8	25.0	56.8	25.5	58.0
80	25.9	58.9	21.4	48.6	23.5	53.4
70	23.2	52.7	19.8	45.0	21.5	48.9
60	21.8	49.5	18.5	42.0	20.4	46.4
50	20.4	46.4	17.0	38.6	19.4	44.1
40	19.4	44.1	15.2	34.5	17.8	40.5
30	18.0	40.9	13.0	29.5	16.8	38.2
20	16.0	36.4	10.0	22.7	15.5	35.2
10	14.0	31.8	8.2	18.6	12.5	28.4
1	7.0	15.9	1.0	2.3	6.0	13.6

* For 88 institutions only; 2 institutions report no teaching laboratory.

tional rooms, while others made the distinction but did not compute the utilization data for all rooms combined.

Table 3 shows the percentile ranking of room-period utilization scores, based on 90 institutions of higher education. The percentile rank of a given utilization score represents the percentage of scores that lie below it. To put it another way, a college with a room-period utilization score of 23.2 periods per week for general classrooms can, on the basis of the data in Table 3, claim that it uses its general classrooms more periods a week on the average than 70 per cent of other institutions of higher education. The median, or 50 percentile point, is 20.4 periods per week for general classrooms. The 99th percentile point is the highest found in this group of institutions, the 1st percentile point is the lowest found.

In addition to the data for average number of periods per week per room, Table 3 also shows the room-period utilization scores expressed as percentages of possible utilization on a 44-hour weekly basis. The average number of periods of room use per week does not mean much unless related to some figure representing a theoretically possible number of periods of use per week. The selection of this theoretically possible figure is arbitrary. One might take 168, the total number of hours in a seven-day week of twenty-four hours each day, as the possible upper limit, and thus report that the average institution uses its general classrooms only 12.1 per cent, or less than one-eighth, of the possible hours such rooms might be used. Somewhat more realistically, suggestion was made earlier that, as a theoretically possible upper limit, an institution might expect to use its classrooms 44 hours a week. This would mean holding classes eight hours a day Monday through Friday and four hours on Saturday morning. Many institutions actually operate their programs on such a schedule, or on even a longer weekly schedule. If the median score (the 50th percentile) for general classrooms, 20.4 periods per week per room, is compared with this theoretically possible use of 44 hours a week, it can be reported that the average institution schedules its classrooms for use only 46 per cent of the possible weekly periods. Or to put it more bluntly, classrooms stand idle more than half the time they might be used.

The median score for teaching laboratories, shown in Table 3, is 17.0 periods per week per room or 38.6 per cent of the theoretically possible utilization of 44 hours a week. For all instructional rooms combined, the median score is 19.4 periods per week per room, or 44.1 per cent of theoretically possible use of 44 hours.

Table 4 shows the percentile ranking of student-station utilization scores, based on 84 institutions. The median score for student-stations in general classrooms is 11.1 hours of use per week

TABLE 4

Percentile Ranking of Student-Station Utilization Scores, Based on 84 Institutions

PERCENTILE RANK	GENERAL CLASSROOMS		TEACHING LABORATORIES *	
	Average Number of Student Hr. per Week per Station	Percentage of Possible Utilization on 44-Hour Weekly Basis	Average Number of Student Hr. per Week per Station	Percentage of Possible Utilization on 44-Hour Weekly Basis
99	25.0	56.8	36.0	81.8
90	17.8	40.5	19.3	43.9
80	15.1	34.3	16.2	36.8
70	13.5	30.7	13.9	31.6
60	12.1	27.5	12.0	27.3
50	11.1	25.2	10.9	24.8
40	9.8	22.3	9.8	22.3
30	9.0	20.5	8.2	18.6
20	8.5	19.3	6.4	14.5
10	6.6	15.0	4.2	9.5
1	3.0	6.8	1.0	2.3

* For 82 institutions only; 2 report no teaching laboratories.

per station, or 25.2 per cent of the possible utilization on a 44-hour weekly basis. For student-stations in teaching laboratories, the median score is 10.9 hours of use per week per station, or 24.8 per cent of the theoretically possible use on a 44-hour week. The data in this tabulation take into account all student-station-periods available, including those hours during which the rooms may have stood idle.

Table 5 presents the percentile ranking of scores for student-station use during the hours the rooms were actually occupied. The median score for general classrooms is 53.3 per cent, and for teaching laboratories, 63.0 per cent. It is apparent from the scores in this tabulation that most institutions construct their instructional rooms considerably larger than necessary for the size of classes scheduled in them. The most effective method of correcting this situation is to increase the average size of classes during a period of enrollment increase. When new instructional facilities are built, the rooms should be designed so that they are better fitted to the size of classes to be housed in them. Otherwise,

TABLE 5

Percentile Ranking of Scores for "Percentage of Student-Stations Used When Rooms Are Actually in Use," Based on 83 Institutions

PERCENTILE RANK	GENERAL CLASSROOMS	TEACHING LABORATORIES*
99	89.0	109.0
90	73.5	82.0
80	65.5	75.5
70	61.5	70.5
60	57.2	67.2
50	53.3	63.0
40	50.0	58.5
30	46.3	55.5
20	43.5	52.5
10	40.8	44.5
1	28.0	39.0

* For 81 institutions; 2 institutions report no teaching laboratory.

this particular form of inefficiency will continue to plague an institution. At the same time care must be taken in planning new facilities to foresee desirable and necessary changes in the distribution of size of classes.

Shortly after these three tabulations were prepared, an opportunity was presented to compare several of the median scores with comparable scores for a group of approximately 25 institutions that had participated in a recently completed state-wide study of plant facilities. The scores from the new group of institutions closely approximated the norms here presented, in several instances being practically identical. Unfortunately the data for the new group of institutions were not in a form that permitted incorporation in the table of norms. This and several other tests made suggest that the median scores reported in Tables 3, 4, and 5 have a high degree of stability. Until more recent data are obtained for a much larger and a more representative sampling of institutions, however, the scores presented in these tabulations should not be accepted as being a final set of normative data.

Institutional Characteristics Associated with Degree of Utilization

Within the limits of the data available from current studies of space utilization, an exploratory attempt was made to identify institutional characteristics that appear to be associated with the degree of utilization. A number of such characteristics have been suggested in various studies. Among them are program differences, institutional locale—especially as to population size of the community, quality of plant facilities, institutional control (private or public), and size of enrollments. The utilization data obtained for the 101 institutions permitted analyses of the possible association of three such factors, size of enrollment, level of program, and institutional control.

SIZE OF INSTITUTION

Data on total number of student-credit-hours produced during the academic year 1953–54, excluding the summer session, were obtained for 41 degree-granting institutions and 30 junior colleges. The space utilization data for each of these 71 institutions are for the fall term of 1953. The student-credit-hour data permitted a grouping of institutions according to size, such as those with a total student-credit-hour production of 16,000 or less, or with 32,000 or more. It is to be remembered that the total number of student-credit-hours produced by an institution is directly related to its full-time-equivalent student enrollment, inasmuch as a full-time student ordinarily earns from 30 to 32 semester hours of credit in an academic year. An institution with a total student-credit-hour production of 16,000 semester hours would thus have an enrollment of approximately 500 full-time-equivalent students.

Table 6 shows the room-period utilization scores for 41 degree-granting institutions, classified by volume of student-credit-hours produced during the academic year 1953–54. The tabulation is divided into three parts. Part A groups the institutions into those with student-credit-hour production of 32,000 or fewer and those with more than 32,000. Part B is based on three groupings, institutions with a student-credit-hour production of 16,000 or fewer, from 16,001 to 48,000, and 48,001 or more. For Table 6, Parts A and B, five scores are shown for each group—the first quartile score (the 25th percentile), the median score (the 50th percentile), the third quartile (the 75th percentile), and the lowest and highest institutional averages to indicate the range. Table 6, Part C, deals with institutions with more than 48,000 student-credit-hours, classified into two size groups. Because of the small number of institutions involved, only the median score and the lowest and highest institutional averages are shown.

The data in Table 6, Part A, show that degree-granting institutions with a total student-credit-hour production of more than 32,000 make far more use of their instructional rooms than smaller institutions. The first quartile scores for "general classrooms" and "all instructional rooms" for the larger institutions are slightly higher than the corresponding third quartile scores for the smaller institutions. In the case of "teaching laboratories," the third quartile scores for the smaller institutions fall between the first quartile and the median scores for the larger institutions. The scores for the median and the first and third quartiles in Table 6, Part B, indicate a definite progression, with the largest institutions having the highest room-period utilization, the middle-sized group the next highest, and the smallest institutions the lowest utilization.

In order to explore the possibility of the continuation of the progression among the 12 institutions with student-credit-hour productions of more than 48,000, these large institutions were

TABLE 6

Room-Period Utilization Scores for Fall 1953 for 41 Institutions Maintaining Programs Leading to the Bachelor's or a Higher Degree, Classified by Volume of Student-Credit-Hours Produced during the Regular Academic Year 1953–54

KIND OF ROOMS	SCORE	AVERAGE NUMBER OF PERIODS PER WEEK PER ROOM IN INSTITUTIONS WITH STUDENT-CREDIT-HOUR PRODUCTION OF:							
		Part A			Part B			Part C	
		1,624 to 410,507 (N=41)*	32,000 or Fewer (N=21)	More than 32,000 (N=20)	16,000 or Fewer (N=15)	16,001 to 48,000 (N=14)	More than 48,000 (N=12)	48,001 to 144,000 (N=7)	More than 144,000 (N=5)
General Classrooms	Highest	38.0	22.0	38.0	22.0	38.0	38.0	37.0	38.0
	Third Quartile	23.8	19.3	27.0	19.8	22.0	29.0	—	—
	Median	19.8	15.9	24.0	15.8	19.0	25.0	26.0	24.0
	First Quartile	15.6	12.8	20.0	10.4	15.8	23.0	—	—
	Lowest	7.0	7.0	15.0	7.0	12.0	20.0	20.0	15.0
Teaching Laboratories	Highest	32.0	21.0	32.0	21.0	18.0	32.0	32.0	21.0
	Third Quartile	17.9	14.9	20.8	14.0	16.0	21.5	—	—
	Median	14.0	10.0	16.5	10.0	12.5	19.5	21.0	16.0
	First Quartile	9.2	8.1	12.0	7.3	9.0	15.5	—	—
	Lowest	5.0	5.0	8.0	5.0	7.0	11.0	15.0	11.0
All Instructional Rooms	Highest	35.0	21.0	35.0	21.0	28.0	35.0	35.0	28.0
	Third Quartile	20.9	17.1	24.0	16.6	19.8	25.0	—	—
	Median	17.4	14.3	20.5	14.0	16.5	22.0	22.0	22.0
	First Quartile	13.6	12.1	18.0	10.3	13.8	19.5	—	—
	Lowest	6.0	6.0	12.0	6.0	12.0	18.0	19.0	18.0

* Number of institutions in each size group.

divided into two groups—those with 48,001 to 144,000 student-credit-hours (from approximately 1,500 to 4,500 full-time-equivalent students) and those with more than 144,000 student-credit-hours (enrollments larger than approximately 4,500 full-time-equivalent students). A comparison of the scores shown in Table 6, Part C, suggests no clear pattern of superior room-period utilization on the part of either group. The number of cases in the two groups, furthermore, is insufficient for any definite conclusions to be drawn from the observed differences in the medians.

Table 7 shows the student-station utilization scores for the fall of 1953 for 38 degree-granting institutions, classified by volume of student-credit-hours produced. This tabulation, like Table 6, is also presented in three parts.

The data in Table 7, Part A, show that, as in the case of room-period utilization, the institutions with student-credit-hour production of more than 32,000 make substantially greater use of student-stations than the smaller institutions. The first quartile scores for the larger institutions are higher than the third quartile scores for the smaller institutions, for each of the three categories of instructional rooms. The scores in Part B of Table 7 indicate a definite progression, with the largest institutions having the highest student-station utilization rates, the middle-size group the next highest, and the smallest institutions the lowest rates. The scores for the 12 largest institutions were divided into two categories, those for institutions with a production of 48,001 to 144,000 student-credit-hours and of more than 144,000 student-credit-hours. The result, presented in Table 7, Part C, suggests that the smaller of these two categories of institutions have slightly higher average rates of student-station utilization, for general classrooms, teaching laboratories, and for all instructional rooms combined. The number of institutions used to make this comparison is so small that, until further tests are made with data based on more institutions, it would be advisable to proceed on the assumption that such differences as might exist among institutions with enrollments larger than approximately 1,500

TABLE 7

Student-Station Utilization Scores for Fall 1953 for 38 Institutions Maintaining Programs Leading to the Bachelor's or a Higher Degree, Classified by Volume of Student-Credit-Hours Produced during the Regular Academic Year 1953–54

AVERAGE NUMBER OF STUDENT HOURS PER WEEK PER STATION IN INSTITUTIONS WITH STUDENT-CREDIT-HOUR PRODUCTION OF:

STUDENT-STATIONS LOCATED IN:	SCORE	Part A			Part B			Part C	
		1,624 to 410,507 (N=38)*	32,000 or Fewer (N=18)	More than 32,000 (N=20)	16,000 or Fewer (N=14)	16,001 to 48,000 (N=12)	More than 48,000 (N=12)	48,001 to 144,000 (N=7)	More than 144,000 (N=5)
General Classrooms	Highest	24.0	10.0	24.0	10.0	18.0	24.0	24.0	17.0
	Third Quartile	12.0	8.9	16.5	8.9	11.0	17.5	—	—
	Median	9.2	7.8	12.2	7.8	9.5	15.0	15.0	13.0
	First Quartile	7.3	5.8	9.5	5.0	7.0	12.0	—	—
	Lowest	3.0	3.0	6.0	3.0	6.0	9.0	9.0	9.0
Teaching Laboratories	Highest	21.0	17.0	21.0	17.0	14.0	21.0	21.0	19.0
	Third Quartile	12.3	8.0	15.0	8.0	10.5	16.5	—	—
	Median	8.5	6.0	11.2	5.5	8.0	14.5	15.0	11.0
	First Quartile	5.4	4.3	9.0	4.0	5.5	11.5	—	—
	Lowest	3.0	3.0	4.0	3.0	4.0	9.0	12.0	9.0
All Instructional Rooms	Highest	22.0	16.0	22.0	16.0	16.0	22.0	22.0	18.0
	Third Quartile	12.3	8.7	15.8	9.0	10.5	16.5	—	—
	Median	9.0	7.8	11.5	7.8	8.5	14.5	15.0	12.0
	First Quartile	7.6	5.3	9.5	4.8	7.5	11.5	—	—
	Lowest	3.0	3.0	6.0	3.0	6.0	9.0	11.0	9.0

* Number of institutions in each size group.

full-time-equivalent students do not warrant the development of a separate set of norms for student-station utilization.

Table 8 shows the scores for station use during the hours that rooms are actually occupied, for 41 degree-granting institutions classified by size. This table, like the two preceding ones, is also presented in three parts.

Part A of Table 8 shows that institutions with a total student-credit-hour production of more than 32,000 have a higher average rate of station use during the hours the rooms are occupied, than the smaller institutions. The differences in scores, however, are not as pronounced as they are for room and student-station-period utilization. The data in Part B of Table 8 suggest a progression, with the smaller institutions generally having lower utilization scores than the next group of larger institutions. The variations in degree of utilization between institutions of 16,000 student-credit-hours or fewer and institutions with from 16,001 to 48,000 student-credit-hours, are not, however, particularly significant.

The median scores in Part C of Table 8 suggest no increase in utilization associated with increase in size, for institutions with student-credit-hour productions of more than 48,000.

It is clear from the foregoing tabulations that institutional size, as measured by the total number of student-credit-hours produced, is definitely associated with the degree of utilization of instructional space among degree-granting institutions. Because of this relationship, it seems advisable to have different sets of utilization norms for each of three size-groups of degree-granting institutions, one set for institutions with a regular academic year production up to 16,000 student-credit-hours, a second set for institutions with student-credit-hour production ranging from 16,001 to 48,000, and a third set for those with more than 48,000 student-credit-hours. Further experimentation with utilization data may indicate that for certain measures of use, particularly the percentage of station-use during the hours rooms are actually occupied, some other grouping for size may be more satisfactory.

TABLE 8

Scores for "Percentage of Student-Stations Used When Rooms Are Actually in Use" for Fall 1953 for 41 Institutions Maintaining Programs Leading to the Bachelor's or a Higher Degree, Classified by Volume of Student-Credit-Hours Produced during the Regular Academic Year 1953–54

STUDENT-STATIONS LOCATED IN:	SCORES	PERCENTAGE OF STUDENT-STATIONS USED WHEN ROOMS ARE ACTUALLY IN USE FOR INSTITUTIONS WITH STUDENT-CREDIT-HOUR PRODUCTION OF:							
		Part A			Part B			Part C	
		1,624 to 410,507 (N=41)*	32,000 or Fewer (N=21)	More than 32,000 (N=20)	16,000 or Fewer (N=15)	16,001 to 48,000 (N=14)	More than 48,000 (N=12)	48,001 to 144,000 (N=7)	More than 144,000 (N=5)
General Classrooms	Highest	72.0	72.0	67.0	72.0	60.0	67.0	67.0	62.0
	Third Quartile	55.8	53.4	57.0	51.5	53.0	61.0	—	—
	Median	48.0	45.0	49.0	42.0	47.0	52.5	57.0	48.0
	First Quartile	41.9	40.8	43.5	36.5	42.0	47.0	—	—
	Lowest	28.0	28.0	29.0	28.0	29.0	43.0	46.0	43.0
Teaching Laboratories	Highest	90.0	90.0	81.0	90.0	70.0	81.0	74.0	81.0
	Third Quartile	68.9	61.3	69.5	62.0	61.0	72.5	—	—
	Median	60.0	55.0	64.0	54.0	54.5	68.0	67.0	65.0
	First Quartile	52.3	50.8	54.0	48.5	49.0	62.5	—	—
	Lowest	41.0	43.0	41.0	43.0	41.0	58.0	58.0	62.0

* Number of institutions in each size group.

Table 9 shows the room-period scores for the fall of 1953 for 30 publicly controlled junior colleges, classified by volume of student-credit-hours produced during the academic year 1953–54.

TABLE 9

Room-Period Utilization Scores for Fall 1953 for 30 Publicly Controlled Junior Colleges, Classified by Volume of Student-Credit-Hours Produced during the Regular Academic Year 1953–54[a]

KIND OF ROOMS	SCORE	AVERAGE NUMBER OF PERIODS PER WEEK PER ROOM IN JUNIOR COLLEGES WITH STUDENT-CREDIT-HOUR PRODUCTION OF:				
		Part A		Part B		
		32,000 or Fewer (N=16)*	More than 32,000 (N=14)	16,000 or Fewer (N=7)	16,001 to 48,000 (N=15)	More than 48,000 (N=8)
General Classrooms	Highest	42.0	27.0	31.0	42.0	27.0
	Third Quartile	22.5	25.0	—	—	—
	Median	21.5	22.0	22.0	20.0	24.5
	First Quartile	18.5	19.0	—	—	—
	Lowest	17.0	11.0	17.0	17.0	11.0
Teaching Laboratories	Highest	31.0	33.0	22.0	31.0	33.0
	Third Quartile	21.5	25.8	—	—	—
	Median	19.5	22.0	19.0	20.0	25.0
	First Quartile	18.0	18.0	—	—	—
	Lowest	14.0	15.0	14.0	15.0	16.0
All Instructional Rooms	Highest	36.0	28.0	25.0	36.0	28.0
	Third Quartile	22.0	26.0	—	—	—
	Median	20.2	22.0	20.0	20.0	25.0
	First Quartile	17.5	19.3	—	—	—
	Lowest	16.0	16.0	16.0	17.0	16.0

[a] Actual SCH production from 8,032 to 113,315.
* Number of institutions in each size group.

These are rather large junior colleges, with enrollments ranging from approximately 250 to 3,500 full-time-equivalent students. The median scores in Table 9, Part A, indicate that the larger junior colleges make a slightly greater use of instructional space than the smaller junior colleges. The scores in Table 9, Part B, suggest that junior colleges with from 8,000 to 16,000 student-credit-hours are, on the average, able to use their instructional rooms as effectively as those with from 16,001 to 48,000 student-

TABLE 10

Student-Station Utilization Scores for Fall 1953 for 30 Publicly Controlled Junior Colleges, Classified by Volume of Student-Credit-Hours Produced during the Regular Academic Year 1953–54[a]

STUDENT-STATIONS LOCATED IN:	SCORE	AVERAGE NUMBER OF HOURS PER WEEK PER STATION IN JUNIOR COLLEGES WITH STUDENT-CREDIT-HOUR PRODUCTION OF:				
		Part A		Part B		
		32,000 or Fewer (N=16)*	More than 32,000 (N=14)	16,000 or Fewer (N=7)	16,001 to 48,000 (N=15)	More than 48,000 (N=8)
General Classrooms	Highest	25.0	20.0	14.0	25.0	20.0
	Third Quartile	13.0	17.3	—	—	—
	Median	11.8	14.5	11.0	12.0	17.0
	First Quartile	10.5	9.5	—	—	—
	Lowest	8.0	9.0	8.0	9.0	9.0
Teaching Laboratories	Highest	21.0	36.0	16.0	21.0	36.0
	Third Quartile	14.3	19.8	—	—	—
	Median	12.5	16.5	10.0	13.3	19.0
	First Quartile	10.5	11.3	—	—	—
	Lowest	6.0	8.0	6.0	8.0	10.0

[a] Actual SCH production range from 8,032 to 113,315.
* Number of institutions in size group.

credit-hours. The median scores for the largest junior colleges, those producing more than 48,000 student-credit-hours annually, are significantly higher than the scores for the smaller institutions.

Table 10 shows the student-station utilization scores for 30 junior colleges, classified by size. The data for student-station utilization for "all instructional rooms" were not obtainable for this group of institutions. The median scores in Part A indicate that the large junior colleges are able to make more intensive use of student-stations than the small institutions. The scores in Part B suggest a definite progression, with the largest junior colleges having the highest rates of student-station utilization, the middle

TABLE 11

Scores for "Percentage of Student-Stations Used When Rooms Are
Actually in Use" for 30 Publicly Controlled Junior Colleges,
Classified by Volume of Student-Credit-Hours Produced
during the Regular Academic Year 1953–54[a]

STUDENT-STATIONS LOCATED IN:	SCORE	PERCENTAGE OF STATIONS USED WHEN ROOMS ARE ACTUALLY IN USE FOR JUNIOR COLLEGES WITH STUDENT-CREDIT-HOUR PRODUCTION OF:				
		Part A		Part B		
		32,000 or Fewer (N = 16)*	More than 32,000 (N = 14)	16,000 or Fewer (N = 7)	16,001 to 48,000 (N = 15)	More than 48,000 (N = 8)
General	Highest	74.0	84.0	62.0	74.0	84.0
Classrooms	Third Quartile	61.5	75.0	—	—	—
	Median	54.3	66.5	52.0	61.3	70.5
	First Quartile	51.0	59.0	—	—	—
	Lowest	42.0	45.0	42.0	45.0	57.0
Teaching	Highest	86.0	109.0	81.0	86.0	109.0
Laboratories	Third Quartile	70.5	77.3	—	—	—
	Median	62.5	72.5	60.0	66.3	73.5
	First Quartile	55.0	65.0	—	—	—
	Lowest	39.0	55.0	39.0	55.0	64.0

[a] Actual SCH production range from 8,032 to 113,315.
* Number of institutions in size group.

group the next highest, and the smallest institutions the lowest scores. The significant difference in median scores occurs between institutions that lie above and below the 48,000 student-credit-hour production level.

Table 11 shows the scores for percentage of student stations used during the hours that rooms are occupied for 30 publicly controlled junior colleges, classified by size. The data in this tabulation suggest a consistent pattern of significant difference in utilization, with the larger institutions having higher rates of use than the smaller institutions.

The data in Tables 9, 10, and 11 indicate that size of enrollment is definitely associated with degree of instructional space use among publicly controlled junior colleges. The data also suggest that the size-groups that might be used to present normative data for space utilization for junior colleges should be different from those recommended for degree-granting institutions. The most suitable dividing point for publicly controlled junior colleges appears to be 48,000 student-credit-hours, or an enrollment of approximately 1,500 full-time-equivalent students. It should be noted, however, that the junior colleges represented in these tabulations do not include privately controlled institutions or those with less than 8,000 student-credit-hours. A separate set of normative data may be advisable for junior colleges with less than 250 full-time-equivalent students, or 8,000 student-credit-hours, especially since many of the junior colleges in this country are of approximately this size. This and the question of the relationship of size to degree of utilization among privately controlled junior colleges are subjects for further research.

INSTITUTIONAL CONTROL

Control, whether public or private, is another institutional characteristic tested for association with the degree of space utilization. Table 12 shows the room-period utilization scores for the fall of 1953 for 41 degree-granting institutions, classified by control and by volume of student-credit-hours produced during the regular academic year 1953–54. Table 13 presents the student-station utilization scores for 38 institutions, classified similarly by control and by size. In both tabulations only the median scores for each size and control group are shown. Because of the small number of institutions for which data were available to make this analysis, only two size-groups were used, those with a student-credit-hour production of more than 32,000 and those with 32,000 or fewer.

The data of Tables 12 and 13 indicate a consistent pattern of difference, with publicly controlled institutions of both size groups having higher rates of utilization than privately controlled institutions of the same size on both room use and student-station

TABLE 12

Room-Period Utilization Scores for Fall 1953 for 41 Institutions Maintaining Programs Leading to the Bachelor's or a Higher Degree, Classified by Control and by Total Number of Student-Credit-Hours Produced during the Regular Academic Year 1953–54

KIND OF INSTRUCTIONAL SPACE	MEDIAN SCORES FOR GROUPS OF INSTITUTIONS WITH:			
	Production of 32,000 SCH or Less		Production of More than 32,000 SCH	
	7 Public[a]	14 Private[b]	15 Public[c]	5 Private[d]
General Classrooms	20.0	15.8	25.8	23.0
Teaching Laboratories	15.0	9.0	18.0	9.0
All Instructional Rooms	17.0	13.2	21.8	18.0

[a] Actual SCH range from 4,927 to 22,330.
[b] Actual SCH range from 1,624 to 31,416.
[c] Actual SCH range from 40,544 so 410,507.
[d] Actual SCH range from 33,530 to 213,523.

use. As an additional test of this relationship, median scores for room and student-station utilization for "all instructional rooms" were derived for 7 publicly controlled and 8 privately controlled degree-granting institutions, each with a student-credit-hour production of more than 16,000 but less than 48,001 during the regular academic year 1953–54. The privately controlled institutions included in this group were composed of several institutions not represented in Tables 12 and 13, and of different geographical location. The median scores again showed a consistent pattern of higher utilization on the part of the publicly controlled institutions. The scores are: for publicly controlled institutions—

room-period utilization 10.0, student-station utilization 19.0; for privately controlled institutions—room-period utilization 7.8, student-station utilization 16.5.

An analysis of the scores for "percentage of student-stations used when rooms are actually in use" for the fall of 1953 for the

TABLE 13

Student-Station Utilization Scores for Fall 1953 for 38 Institutions Maintaining Programs Leading to the Bachelor's or a Higher Degree, Classified by Control and by Total Student-Credit-Hours Produced during the Regular Academic Year 1953–54

KIND OF INSTRUCTIONAL SPACE	MEDIAN SCORES FOR FOLLOWING GROUPS OF INSTITUTIONS:			
	Production of 32,000 SCH or Less		Production of More than 32,000 SCH	
	7 Public[a]	11 Private[b]	15 Public[c]	5 Private[d]
Student Stations in General Classrooms	8.7	7.3	14.8	10.0
Student Stations in Teaching Laboratories	8.0	5.0	11.9	6.0
Student Stations in All Instructional Rooms	8.3	7.6	14.0	9.0

[a] Actual SCH range from 4,927 to 22,330.
[b] Actual SCH range from 1,624 to 31,416.
[c] Actual SCH range from 40,544 to 410,507.
[d] Actual SCH range from 33,530 to 213,523.

41 degree-granting institutions, classified by volume of student-credit-hour production and by control, revealed no consistent pattern of significant difference between publicly controlled and privately controlled institutions. The results are shown in Table 14.

The data in Tables 12 and 13 suggest that it would be advisable to develop different sets of norms for publicly controlled and privately controlled degree-granting institutions of each size group. There appears to be a significant and consistent difference in room use and student-station use, between publicly controlled and privately controlled institutions of comparable size. The data in Table 14, on percentage of stations used during the hours rooms are occupied, indicate that different sets of norms for

TABLE 14

Scores for "Percentage of Student-Stations Used When Rooms Are Actually in Use" for Fall 1953 for 41 Institutions Maintaining Programs Leading to the Bachelor's or a Higher Degree, Classified by Control and by Volume of Student-Credit-Hours Produced during the Regular Academic Year 1953–54

	PERCENTAGE OF STUDENT STATIONS USED WHEN ROOMS ARE ACTUALLY IN USE							
	Institutions with Student-Credit-Hour Production of 32,000 or Fewer				Institutions with Student-Credit-Hour Production of More Than 32,000			
	7 Public Institutions		14 Private Institutions		15 Public Institutions		5 Private Institutions	
	General Class-rooms	Teaching Labora-tories	General Class-rooms	Teaching Labora-tories	General Class-rooms	Teaching Labora-tories	General Class-rooms	Teaching Labora-tories
Highest Institu-tional Average	53.0	76.0	72.0	90.0	67.0	81.0	56.0	76.0
Median	42.0	53.0	47.0	55.0	50.0	67.0	48.0	54.0
Lowest Institu-tional Average	33.0	45.0	28.0	43.0	29.0	44.0	41.0	41.0

publicly controlled and privately controlled degree-granting institutions are not necessary.

LEVEL OF PROGRAM

A third institutional characteristic tested for possible association with degree of utilization of instructional rooms was the level of program. This analysis was limited to a comparison of utilization scores for degree-granting institutions and junior colleges.

Tables 15, 16, and 17 show the percentile ranking of scores for degree-granting institutions, respectively, for room-period utilization, for student-station utilization, and for percentage of station-use during the hours rooms are actually occupied. The data in each of these tabulations may be considered as tentative norms for each of these three measures of utilization, for degree-granting institutions.

Table 18 shows the percentile ranking of room-period utilization scores, based on 33 public junior colleges. Table 19 presents

TABLE 15

Percentile Ranking of Room-Period Utilization Scores, Based on 57 Institutions Maintaining Programs Leading to the Bachelor's or a Higher Degree

PER-CENTILE RANK	GENERAL CLASSROOMS		TEACHING LABORATORIES*		ALL INSTRUCTIONAL ROOMS	
	Average Number of Periods per Week per Room	Percentage of Possible Utilization on 44-Hour Weekly Basis	Average Number of Periods per Week per Room	Percentage of Possible Utilization on 44-Hour Weekly Basis	Average Number of Periods per Week per Room	Percentage of Possible Utilization on 44-Hour Weekly Basis
99	38.0	86.4	32.0	72.7	35.0	79.5
90	28.8	65.5	21.0	47.7	24.8	56.4
80	26.0	59.1	18.3	41.6	21.7	49.3
70	23.2	52.7	16.7	38.0	20.3	46.1
60	21.2	48.2	15.1	34.3	19.1	43.4
50	19.9	45.2	13.2	30.0	17.4	39.5
40	18.9	43.0	11.8	26.8	16.6	37.7
30	16.3	37.0	9.8	22.3	15.0	34.1
20	14.8	33.6	8.7	19.8	13.3	30.2
10	12.3	28.0	7.0	15.9	11.2	25.5
1	7.0	15.9	1.0	2.3	6.0	13.6

* For 55 institutions only; 2 institutions report no teaching laboratory.

a similar ranking of scores for student-station-period utilization and for percentage of stations used when rooms are actually occupied, for the same group of junior colleges. These data may be used as tentative norms for this level of institutions.

A comparison of the percentile scores in Tables 15, 16, and 17 with the comparable scores in Tables 18 and 19 indicates that public junior colleges tend to have significantly higher rates of utilization than the degree-granting institutions, on each of the

TABLE 16

Percentile Ranking of Student-Station Utilization Scores, Based on 51 Institutions Maintaining Programs Leading to the Bachelor's or a Higher Degree

PER-CENTILE RANK	GENERAL CLASSROOMS		TEACHING LABORATORIES*		ALL INSTRUCTIONAL ROOMS	
	Average Number of Student Hours per Week per Station	Percentage of Possible Utilization on 44-Hour Weekly Basis	Average Number of Student Hours per Week per Station	Percentage of Possible Utilization on 44-Hour Weekly Basis	Average Number of Student Hours per Week per Station	Percentage of Possible Utilization on 44-Hour Weekly Basis
99	24.0	54.5	21.0	47.7	22.0	50.0
90	16.4	37.3	16.1	36.6	15.7	35.7
80	13.7	31.1	12.7	28.9	13.1	29.8
70	12.0	27.3	11.2	25.5	11.7	26.6
60	10.6	24.1	10.0	22.7	10.8	24.5
50	9.6	21.8	8.6	19.5	9.6	21.8
40	9.1	20.7	7.6	17.3	8.8	20.0
30	8.3	18.9	5.7	13.0	8.1	18.4
20	7.1	16.1	4.7	10.7	7.1	16.1
10	5.5	12.5	3.3	7.5	5.1	11.6
1	3.0	6.8	1.0	2.3	3.0	6.8

* 49 institutions only; 2 report no teaching laboratories.

TABLE 17

Percentile Ranking of Scores for "Percentage of Student-Stations Used When Rooms Are Actually in Use," Based on 50 Institutions Maintaining Programs Leading to the Bachelor's or a Higher Degree

PERCENTILE RANK	GENERAL CLASSROOMS	TEACHING LABORATORIES*
99	74.0	100.0
90	65.5	76.0
80	59.8	70.0
70	54.0	68.0
60	51.8	62.5
50	48.5	59.5
40	46.0	55.5
30	43.0	52.5
20	41.3	49.5
10	38.0	43.8
1	28.0	41.0

* For 48 institutions only; 2 institutions report no teaching laboratory.

three measures of space use. In view of the foregoing findings relating to the association of institutional control and size to degree of utilization, an analysis was made of the scores of public degree-granting institutions and public junior colleges of comparable size groups. The results are shown in Table 20. Only the median scores for each group of institutions are presented.

TABLE 18

Percentile Ranking of Room-Period Utilization Scores for Fall 1953 for 33 Publicly Controlled Junior Colleges, Each Having Sole Use of Its Plant

PER-CENTILE RANK	GENERAL CLASSROOMS		TEACHING LABORATORIES		ALL INSTRUCTIONAL ROOMS	
	Average Number of Periods per Week per Room	Percentage of Possible Utilization on 44-Hour Weekly Basis	Average Number of Periods per Week per Room	Percentage of Possible Utilization on 44-Hour Weekly Basis	Average Number of Periods per Week per Room	Percentage of Possible Utilization on 44-Hour Weekly Basis
99	42.0	95.5	33.0	75.0	36.0	81.8
90	27.2	61.8	30.0	68.2	27.0	61.4
80	25.5	58.0	26.0	59.1	24.3	55.2
70	23.2	52.7	22.5	51.1	23.7	53.9
60	22.3	50.7	21.8	49.5	22.5	51.1
50	21.2	48.2	20.5	46.6	21.1	48.0
40	20.3	46.1	19.5	44.3	20.3	46.1
30	19.5	44.3	18.9	43.0	19.5	44.3
20	18.0	40.9	17.5	39.8	18.5	42.0
10	16.5	37.5	15.5	35.2	16.8	38.2
1	11.0	25.0	14.0	31.8	16.0	36.4

The scores in Table 20 indicate that, while the pattern is not consistent on all measures and for all kinds of instructional space and for all size groups, the publicly controlled junior colleges tend to have somewhat higher rates of utilization than the publicly controlled degree-granting institutions of comparable size. The variations in room-period utilization scores are not particularly significant, except that the publicly controlled junior colleges appear to have a consistently higher rate of use of teaching laboratories than the publicly controlled degree-granting institutions in all size categories. The junior colleges tend to exceed the publicly controlled degree-granting institutions in rate of student-station utilization when rooms are in use. The junior colleges con-

TABLE 19

Percentile Ranking of Scores for Student-Station-Period Utilization and for "Percentage of Student-Stations Used When Rooms Are Actually in Use," Based on 33 Publicly Controlled Junior Colleges, Each Having Sole Use of Its Plant

PER-CENTILE RANK	STUDENT-STATION-PERIOD USE				PERCENTAGE OF STATIONS USED WHEN ROOMS ARE ACTUALLY OCCUPIED	
	General Classrooms		Teaching Laboratories		General Class-rooms	Teaching Labora-tories
	Average Number of Student Hours per Week per Station	Percentage of Possible Utilization on 44-Hour Weekly Basis	Average Number of Student Hours per Week per Station	Percentage of Possible Utilization on 44-Hour Weekly Basis		
99	25.0	56.8	36.0	81.8	89.0	109.0
90	19.2	43.6	22.2	50.5	78.0	85.8
80	17.0	38.6	18.9	43.0	73.5	78.5
70	15.1	34.3	17.1	38.9	68.5	75.0
60	13.8	31.4	14.5	33.0	63.5	72.0
50	12.4	28.2	13.8	31.4	62.3	67.0
40	11.9	27.0	12.6	28.6	59.0	64.5
30	11.1	25.2	11.4	25.9	54.2	61.0
20	9.4	21.4	10.7	24.3	52.5	56.8
10	8.9	20.2	8.6	19.5	45.8	54.8
1	8.0	18.2	6.0	13.6	42.0	39.0

sistently have a higher rate of student-station utilization of teaching laboratories than the publicly controlled degree-granting institutions have, but there is no consistent difference in the station use of general classrooms in the two groups of institutions. It must be remembered that the number of cases included in Table 20 is too small to permit final conclusions, but the data do suggest the advisability of developing different sets of norms for publicly controlled junior colleges and publicly controlled degree-granting institutions.

TABLE 20

Instructional Space Utilization Scores for Fall 1953 for Publicly Controlled Degree-granting Institutions and Publicly Controlled Junior Colleges, Classified by Volume of Student-Credit-Hours Produced during the Regular Academic Year 1953–54

	32,000 SCH OR FEWER		MORE THAN 32,000 SCH		10,500 TO 72,500 SCH	
	7 Public Degree-granting Institutions	16 Public Junior Colleges	15 Public Degree-granting Institutions	14 Public Junior Colleges	12 Public Degree-granting Institutions	27 Public Junior Colleges
Room-Period Utilization, Median Scores:						
General Classrooms	20.0	21.5	25.8	22.0	20.5	20.8
Teaching Laboratories	15.0	19.5	18.0	22.0	17.5	19.9
All Instr. Rooms	17.0	20.2	21.8	22.0	20.3	20.6
Student-Station Utilization, Median Scores:						
General Classrooms	8.7	11.8	14.8	14.5	10.0	11.8
Teaching Laboratories	8.0	12.5	11.9	16.5	10.5	13.6
Percentage of Stations Used during Hours Rooms Occupied, Median Scores:						
General Classrooms	42.0	54.3	50.0	66.5	44.5	61.3
Teaching Laboratories	53.0	62.5	67.0	72.5	56.5	67.0

Limitations of the Present Analysis and Needs for Further Research

The data in this chapter represent only a beginning effort to formulate a set of comprehensive norms for the utilization of instructional space. The number of recent and comparable studies of plant space utilization in institutions of higher education available for the development of norms was found to be too limited for entirely satisfactory results. Such tests of the tabulations as could be made, however, indicate that the normative data here presented are remarkably stable. Additions of new groups of institutional tabulations did not change the percentile points appreciably.

The analysis in this chapter has investigated three institutional characteristics that might be suspected of being related to the degree of use of instructional space. The evidence is not completely conclusive because of the limited number of institutions for which data were available. The indication, however, is for a need for separate sets of norms for institutions classified according to size, according to kind of control, and according to level of program. Further research is needed to establish the validity of these tentative findings. Further exploration should also be made of other institutional characteristics that may be associated with the degree of utilization of space.

The analysis in this chapter is limited to reports of the utilization of two kinds of instructional space, general classrooms and teaching laboratories, and to a combination of these two. The analysis is further limited to the number of weekly periods of room use and student-station use. A sufficient number of institutional reports were not available to develop norms for other kinds of plant space, or for other measures of utilization such as those based on square feet of floor space. If comparable data could be assembled from a substantial number of institutions, it would be highly desirable to develop norms for many different kinds of floor space, such as square feet of faculty office space per faculty member, square feet of dormitory space per occupant, square feet of library space per student, etc. For many kinds of plant space it may be necessary to invent new measures of utilization. For example, at present there appears to be no suitable method of analyzing the use of research laboratories.

The normative data presented in this chapter refer to conditions in a limited time period, mostly centering around the fall term of 1953. It is entirely possible that the norms here presented are already out of date at the time of their publication. The writers of this *Manual* have found no research showing trends in the use of plant space over a long period of years in any substantial group of institutions. Possibly the pattern of use of instructional space is a rather fixed characteristic of individual institutions. More probably, the expansion in enrollments, that began in the early 1950's and is expected to continue at an accelerated rate at least through 1975, will force many institutions to increase considerably the utilization of their plant space.

Perhaps the most important suggestion that can be made, in concluding this *Manual*, is that the normative data here presented need to be freshened up periodically by new compilations of recent institutional analyses of space utilization. These norms need to be extended to include a larger number of institutions, and to involve other kinds of utilization data than the limited presentation that has been possible at this writing. It is sincerely hoped that the definitions set up in this *Manual*, the procedures that are outlined, and the forms that are presented for gathering and analyzing data, will encourage many institutions to undertake studies of the utilization of their plant space. It is further hoped that such institutions may furnish their data to some central agency for compilation into an improved set of norms. A continuing project for the compilation of normative data on utilization of plant space is earnestly recommended as a worthy enterprise for some organization interested in the effective and efficient operation of institutional programs of higher education.

Index

PUBLICATIONS OF THE
AMERICAN ASSOCIATION OF COLLEGIATE
REGISTRARS AND ADMISSIONS OFFICERS

Requests for any of the following publications may be addressed either to the person indicated, or to the Secretary of the Association, Miss Florence Brady, Occidental College, Los Angeles 41, California.

1. COLLEGE AND UNIVERSITY, the Journal of AACRAO. The current volume is Volume 32. Many back numbers are out of print, but others are obtainable. $1.00 each (50¢ to members of the Association). Address inquiries to E. Vincent O'Brien, Treasurer of AACRAO, Fordham University, 302 Broadway, New York 7, New York.

2. *Topical Index* of COLLEGE AND UNIVERSITY and its predecessors (*Proceedings*, 1910–1924; *Bulletin*, 1926–1937; *Journal*, 1937–1947) through Vol. 25. (Volumes 26 ff are indexed in the Summer issue of each year.) Address the Editor at the Office of Dean of the College, Cedar Crest College, Allentown, Pennsylvania.

3. *An Adequate Transcript Guide*, 1952 Revision. The Association's official guide to the preparation of an acceptable transcript. Howard Shontz, University of California, Davis.

4. *Report of Credit Given*. A summary report of accreditation policies by states. Published annually. Ted McCarrel, University of Iowa, Iowa City. ($1.00 per copy.)

5. *AACRAO Policies and Procedures* (A Handbook). D. T. Ordeman, Oregon State College, Corvallis. $1.00 with order.

6. *College Age Population Trends, 1940–1970*. Ronald B. Thompson, Ohio State University, Columbus.

7. *The Impending Tidal Wave of Students*. Ronald B. Thompson, Ohio State University, Columbus.

8. *Machine Equipment for Efficient Office Operation*. Nelson M. Parkhurst, Purdue University, W. Lafayette, Ind. ($1.00 per copy.)

9. *Professional Training Recommended for the Registrar and Admissions Officer*. Ellen L. Deering, College of the Pacific, Stockton, California.

10. *Secondary School—College Co-operation: an Obligation to Youth*. Clyde Vroman, University of Michigan, Ann Arbor. (35¢ per copy; 30¢ if ordered in lots over 25.)

11. *A Glossary of Terms Used by Registrars and Admissions Officers*. Robert E. Mahn, Ohio University, Athens. ($1.00 per copy).
12. *Know Your AACRAO*. Alfred Thomas, Jr., Arizona State College, Tempe.
13. World Education Series: *Do-It-Yourself Evaluation of Foreign Student Credentials; Germany: A Guide to the Academic Placement of German Students in United States Educational Institutions; Canada: A Guide to the Academic Placement of Canadian Students in United States Educational Institutions*. William H. Strain, Indiana University, Bloomington. (*Germany and Canada*, $1.00 per copy; *Do-It-Yourself*, single copies no charge, larger orders 25¢ per copy.)
14. *Manual for Studies of Space Utilization in Colleges and Universities*, by John Dale Russell and James I. Doi. Order from Robert Mahn, Registrar, Ohio University, Athens, Ohio ($2.00 per copy).